# Embracing Uncertainty

# Embracing Uncertainty

*Breakthrough Methods for Achieving Peace*

*of Mind When Facing the Unknown*

∞

Susan Jeffers, PH.D.

ST. MARTIN'S PRESS ❧ NEW YORK

EMBRACING UNCERTAINTY. Copyright © 2003 by Susan Jeffers, Ph.D. All rights reserved. Printed in the United States of America. No part of this book may be used or reproduced in any manner whatsoever without written permission except in the case of brief quotations embodied in critical articles or reviews. For information, address St. Martin's Press, 175 Fifth Avenue, New York, N.Y. 10010.

www.stmartins.com

*Book design by Richard Oriolo*

Library of Congress Cataloging-in-Publication Data

Jeffers, Susan J.
    Embracing uncertainty : breakthrough methods for achieving peace of mind when facing the unknown / Susan Jeffers.
        p. cm.
    Includes bibliographical references (page 277).
    ISBN 0-312-30955-4
        1. Uncertainty—Psychological aspects. 2. Quality of life—Psychological aspects. I. Title.

BF463.U5 J44 2003
158.1—dc21

                                            2002190898

This book was originally published by Hodder and Stoughton, a division of Hodder Headline, in the United Kingdom.

First U.S. Edition: March 2003

10  9  8  7  6  5  4  3  2  1

*To the many heroes in our world who show us what embracing uncertainty truly looks like.*

*They open our eyes to the astonishing, but sometimes forgotten, strength that lives within us all.*

*We need only to remember.*

# Contents

# Acknowledgments

Life is uncertain, no doubt about it. But one thing is certain . . . I owe my heartfelt thanks to the following people, who each in his or her own way has contributed to making my life so rich and making this book a reality:

Dominick Abel, my American agent, who believes in me and makes it all happen. We've been together a long time and I can always count on him to offer me comfort and encouragement when needed.

Jennifer Enderlin, my wonderful editor at St. Martin's Press, who makes the publishing process a joy. I thank her for seeing the value in this book and for her continuing support. Both are truly appreciated.

SueEllen and Tom Strapp of Powersource, my webmasters extraordinaire! Every time I log on to my website, I smile. I've so enjoyed getting to know them and I am very appreciative of all their efforts on my behalf.

My loyal supporters who buy my books, come to hear me speak, and tell me that I have helped them in some way. How privileged I feel to have been able to connect with so many of you in such a wonderful way!

My dear friends: Donna Gradstein, who carefully read the manuscript and, as always, made valuable suggestions. Paul Huson, author of *How to Test and Develop Your ESP*, who reviewed my chapter on "Increasing the Odds." Thank goodness I passed with flying colors! Jerry Beckerman, who, during our "play dates" while enjoying a cappuccino and a great view, always gives me valuable ways of looking at this world. Chas Eisner, whose spirit in embracing the uncertainty relative to cancer is a lesson for us all. Bill Bast, Lois Luger, Henry Gradstein, Melissa Oberon, John Levoff, Gene Schwam, Myrna Schwam, Jennie Blackton, Ed Philhower, Stewart Copeland, Fiona Copeland, Dick Lobo, Caren Lobo, Terry Robinson, Ken Robinson, Larry Gershman, Anita Gershman, Trevor Chenery, Sue Chenery, Joy Starr, and Mandi Robbins, who support me in a multitude of different ways.

Dr. Renata Mihalic and Dr. Michael Galitzer, who gave me back my health and taught me to see the relationship between my body, mind, and soul in an entirely different light.

My wonderful family: Gerry Gershman, Leslie Wandmacher, and stepchildren, Alice Shelmerdine and Guy Shelmerdine and their loved ones, Michael Wandmacher, Anthony Shelmerdine, and Ashley Jacobs. My very lovable sister, Marcia, and brother-in-law, Bruce Rabiner, who fill my life with laughter and love. (For those keeping track, Bruce is husband number 4 and Marcia's long-lost love. I'm so happy they are together at last.)

And most important, my precious husband, Mark Shelmerdine, my dearest friend in all this world, who makes me feel beautiful, loved, and appreciated. I feel blessed beyond words.

embrace it all embrace it all embrace it all embrace it all embrace it all embrace it all embrace it all embrace it all embrace it all embrace it all embrace it all embrace it all embrace it all embrace it all embrace it all embrace it all embrace it all embrace it all embrace it all embrace it all embrace it all embrace it all **embrace it all** embrace it all embrace it all embrace it all embrace it all embrace it all embrace it all embrace it all embrace it all embrace it all embrace it all embrace it all embrace it all embrace it all embrace it all embrace it all embrace it all embrace it all embrace it all embrace it all embrace it all embrace it all embrace it all embrace it all embrace it all embrace it all embrace it all embrace it all embrace it all embrace it all embrace it all embrace it all embrace it all embrace it all embrace it all embrace it all embrace it all embrace it all embrace it all embrace it all embrace it all embrace it all embrace it all embrace it all **embrace it all** embrace it all embrace it all embrace it all embrace it all embrace it all embrace it all embrace it all embrace it all embrace it all embrace it all embrace it all embrace it all embrace it all embrace it all embrace it all embrace it all embrace it all embrace it all embrace it all embrace it all embrace it all **embrace it all** embrace it all embrace it all embrace it all embrace it all embrace it all embrace it all embrace it all embrace it all embrace it all embrace it all embrace it all embrace it all embrace it all embrace it all embrace it all embrace it all embrace it all embrace it all embrace it all embrace it all embrace it all embrace it all embrace it all **embrace**

# Introduction
# How Do You Choose to Live?

∞

*Now, more than ever, we need something*
*enduring to hold close, something that won't*
*wash away in the furious tides of change.*

—WALTER COOPER[1]

*Embracing Uncertainty* is a book about sleeping better at night . . . about easing the pain in our brains that comes from trying to control the uncontrollable . . . about making life more an enriching adventure than a continuous worry. It is about providing that "something enduring to hold close, something that won't wash away in the furious tides of change."

The wise philosopher, Alan Watts, points out that there is *the feeling* that we live in a time of *unusual* insecurity. He attributes this feeling to the many new technologies with which science and industry are bombarding us. He also attributes it to the many long-held traditions that have broken down relative to family life, religion, and the world of work.[2] Now here's the surprise . . . *Watts made these observations in 1951!*

I would venture to say that the feeling of insecurity has greatly escalated since those seemingly "good old days"! Since then we have lived through many events that have further eroded our sense of security, none more startling and upsetting than the destruction by terrorists of the World Trade Center in New York City and the Pentagon in Washington on September 11, 2001. So many people from all over the world lost their lives. And so many lost people they dearly loved. What happened on this historic day has had the effect of putting the entire world on a state of alert. For how long? Only time will tell.*

To compound the difficulty, we live in a society that teaches us to grasp for control, total control, of everything—our careers, our relationships, our children, our health, our money, the state of the world, and on and on and on. We insist that life be secure, safe, predictable, and all good things. As a result, we are uncomfortable, even panicked, about all the uncertainty in our lives. After all, uncertainty implies "no-control."**

If the truth be told, most of us don't handle this reality of "no-control" very well. We take pills to lessen the anxiety. Or

*This horrific terrorist attack took place just as I was completing this book. I remember thinking to myself that if there was ever a time when the world needed to learn how to embrace uncertainty, this was certainly it.
**The sense in which I am using uncertainty throughout this book is the state of not-knowing what the future holds in any area of our lives . . . or our world.

we go into denial. Or we become addicted to work. Or whatever else we find to do to take our minds off the fact that we have so little control. Or we simply live with a cloud of anxiety that never goes away as we think about the unknown . . . the unexpected . . . and the uncontrollable. What is lamentable about the situation is that . . .

We spend so much of our lives worrying and trying to prevent the bad from happening, that we forget to enjoy the good. What a waste of a life!

Thankfully, it doesn't have to be that way. We don't have to walk around with a dark cloud over our heads. The truth is . . .

Nowhere has it been proven that a rich, joyous, abundant life cannot exist in the presence of uncertainty.

This is a very essential concept for you to take in. There have been many before us and there are many with us today who have proven that life can be wonderful, despite the uncertainty. In fact, there are those who have proven that life can be wonderful because of the uncertainty! *Yes, because of the uncertainty.*

The question is, "What do we need to do to reach this wonderful state of being in this world?" As I pondered this question over and over again prior to and during the writing of this book, I came up with many answers to help you learn how to make life grand despite, better yet, *because of,* the uncertainty.

But before you delve into all the ideas I provide within

these pages, you need to embrace three important realities. Without an understanding and acceptance of these three realities, it is very difficult, if not impossible, to make yourself comfortable with all the uncertainty in the world today. Once you embrace these three realities, you will be on a stronger footing to begin to embrace the grand adventure of it all. And it truly is a grand adventure.

I suggest you read these three realities a number of times. In the beginning, you may not like all of what you read, but ultimately you will be able to see the definite advantages that can come from embracing all the uncertainty in your life.

## Reality 1

*The only certainty is that life is uncertain!*

"Susan, I already know that!" Of course, you already know that. But on a very deep level of your being *you don't truly believe it* . . . nor do you want to believe it! When you picked up this book, the likelihood was that you would have preferred that the title of the book be *Erasing Uncertainty* instead of *Embracing Uncertainty*!

On a very deep level of your being, you want guarantees. Isn't that true? You want a promise that life will give you a happy marriage, lots of money, vigorous health, well-behaved, happy children, a world without conflict . . . or whatever it is for you. If you truly believed that life is uncertain, you wouldn't be looking for any guarantees; you would be looking for something else. And I will keep you in suspense for a little while before I tell you exactly what that something else is.

Again, and I can't repeat it often enough, the reality is that there is never a way to erase the uncertainty in any area of our lives. Name it, and it is uncertain. We could cry, scream, and be angry about this, but nothing is going to change the fact that, even if we do our very best, we cannot predict or control, even the next second of our lives, let alone how our children turn out, how our relationships will turn out, how we are treated at work, how long we will live, and on and on and on.

> There's *nothing* that's certain . . . of THAT you can be certain!

I can hear many of you saying, "How depressing! You mean I REALLY can't control my world? I REALLY can't create the guarantee, the safety, the comfort, I am seeking? I REALLY can't become strong enough to control my own destiny?" My answer is, "No. You cannot gain the kind of control you are seeking."

"Oh, yes, I can, Susan. I can get insurance. I can raise my kids a certain way. I can eat the right food." Denial. Denial. Denial. Of course you can do all of the above and I am not against your taking such action. In fact, I *encourage* it. That still doesn't offer any assurance that things will turn out the way you want them to. The hard reality is that the insurance company can go out of business, your children can grow up the opposite of what you would have wished, and the right food today is the wrong food tomorrow. Whoops! You get the picture.

It is now time for you to take a deep breath and SURREN-
DER to the fact that you can control NOTHING when it
comes to the future. To help you accept this reality, you need
to say to yourself over and over again,

> I have no control over the future.
> I have no control over the future.
> I have no control over the future.

Believe it or not, you will soon come to realize that this
"negative" statement is a very positive affirmation!* As you
repeat this affirmation over and over again, you will consciously LET GO of any hope that you can create any certainty in your life. This sounds like bad news, but it truly
isn't . . . which leads us to the second reality . . .

## Reality 2

*Once you surrender to the fact that you are unable to
control the uncertainty, you will, at last, be able
to breathe a sigh of relief.*

Yes, when you finally do reach that state of SURRENDER,
you can't help but feel the peace that comes when you
stop trying to do the impossible. (Did you ever notice how

---

*Generally speaking, affirmations are best stated as a positive rather than as a
negative. However, there are exceptions to this rule that can serve us in some way.
This is one of those exceptions.

great it feels when you stop hitting your head against the wall?)

Understand that surrender in this case doesn't mean giving up on your attempts to do the very best that you can; it means letting go of something over which you have no control . . . THE OUTCOME of any situation in your life. Once you've let go of the outcome, you can understand why you are overcome with a wonderful sense of calm. "Whew! I don't have to work so hard doing the impossible . . . controlling the future. I can rest at last." What a relief!

*This is important:* As long as you think you can *beat* the very nature of life itself, you avoid looking for a way of being in this world that actually *embraces* the nature of life itself . . . which is uncertainty. You continue to live with the delusion that there has to be a way to control everything.

If, however, you are totally clear that there is no way to create certainty in your life, you can then move on to something more life-affirming. That is, you can learn how to embrace uncertainty instead of trying to *erase* it . . . which, of course, is impossible. Now on to the good news . . .

## Reality 3

*A "deep" acceptance that life is uncertain opens the door to a powerful way of living.*

Earlier, I told you that, if we truly accepted the fact that life was uncertain, we wouldn't be looking for guarantees. We would be looking for something else. And not to keep you in suspense a moment longer, here is what we would be looking for . . .

We would be looking for the valuable gifts inherent in all that happens to us . . . no matter how bad things may seem in any given moment. Finding the gifts minimizes—*even erases*—the suffering.

We would be looking for a way of being in the world that assures us that we could handle whatever life hands us. Therefore, we would live with a "bring it all on!" attitude knowing that we are prepared for anything that comes our way!

We would be looking for a way of being in the world that allows us to see uncertainty, not as something to fear, but as an enriching aspect of life.

Let me tell you a little about my own experience of learning how to embrace uncertainty. I grew up desperately wanting guarantees in my life. I kept looking to Daddy, or Mommy, or God, to always keep me safe and secure. I married very early (at the age of eighteen) hoping that my Prince Charming would make me feel safe and secure. Poor guy! Of course, he couldn't make my fairy-tale expectations come true. This disappointment created a lot of strong emotions within me . . . anger, denial, frustration, helplessness, sadness, and fear. Ultimately, we divorced. Between my marriages, I dated a lot of men, but finally had to admit to myself that there truly was no one out there who could make me feel safe and secure.

So I took another tack. I became defiant and tried to control the uncertainty all by myself. Exhausting . . . and, of course, futile. Ultimately, I had to SURRENDER to the fact that even I, as hard as I tried, couldn't keep the harsh realities of life from knocking at my door . . . realities like illness, or divorce, or the death of people I loved. I was totally helpless when it came to creating certainty in my life.

In the beginning, this realization was very distressing to me. But little by little, as I explored the many ways of accessing the great power that lies within my being, my feelings of distress turned into feelings of delight and discovery. As I learned, and as I wish to convey to you throughout this book . . .

There is great adventure in the unknown that propels us to discover powerful parts of ourselves that we didn't know were there.

Each moment, each day, each age, each experience— good or bad—brings its own challenge and its own wonderment as to how it will all unfold. The trick is to learn to love the uncertainty of it all . . . to find, at last, the great satisfaction, the great joy, and the great opportunity that lies within the uncertainty.

So how do you choose to live? Do you choose to live in a state of unhappiness, exhaustion, and futility . . . or do you choose to live with a sense of excitement and possibility about all the uncertainty in our lives? Yes, you definitely have the choice, and, unless you are a masochist, I am sure you will choose the latter.

Making the choice to live a life filled with excitement and possibility is a first step. Helping you take the next step . . . and the next . . . and the next . . . is what *Embracing Uncertainty* is all about.

In addition to the many new ideas presented within this book, I've included forty-two exercises (yes, forty-two exercises!) to help you get rid of your soul-destroying ways of thinking and being in this world. You would be wise to take note of those particular exercises that "speak" to you as you read through the book. Then go back to your favorite exercises, and little by little, make them an important (and enjoyable) part of your daily life. Eventually, you will be able to embrace the fact that life is grand despite the fact that . . . or better yet, *because* life is uncertain.

I also want you to know that *this book definitely has a mind of its own*! It told me that it wants to be read over and over again. It wants to be your resource when you need help in pushing through your worries about the future. It wants to help you in a multitude of ways. So I suggest that you make this book one of your very best friends. Visit it often and get to know it well. If you do, it won't let you down.

So, are you ready for an adventure of the most exciting kind . . . the kind that propels you from one way of seeing the world into another? As you travel through this book, you will take a magical journey into the mind and into the spirit. Along the way, you will open your eyes to the beauty, the miracle, the joy, and the possibility in it all. All you have to do is take a good seat in the theater and let the story unfold. And what an amazing story it is!

**wonder-full** wonder-full wonder-full wonder-full wonder-full wonder-full wonder-full wonder-full wonder-full wonder-full wonder-full wonder-full wonder-full wonder-full wonder-full wonder-full wonder-full wonder-full wonder-full wonder-full wonder-full wonder-full wonder-full wonder-full wonder-full wonder-full wonder-full wonder-full wonder-full wonder-full wonder-full wonder-full wonder-full wonder-full wonder-full wonder-full wonder-full wonder-full wonder-full wonder-full wonder-full wonder-full wonder-full wonder-full **wonder-full** wonder-full wonder-full wonder-full wonder-full wonder-full wonder-full wonder-full wonder-full wonder-full wonder-full wonder-full wonder-full wonder-full wonder-full wonder-full wonder-full wonder-full wonder-full wonder-full wonder-full wonder-full wonder-full wonder-full wonder-full wonder-full wonder-full wonder-full wonder-full wonder-full wonder-full wonder-full wonder-full wonder-full wonder-full wonder-full wonder-full wonder-full wonder-full full **wonder-full** wonder-full wonder-full wonder-full wonder-full wonder-full wonder-full wonder-full wonder-full wonder-full wonder-full wonder-full wonder-full wonder-full wonder-full wonder-full wonder-full wonder-full wonder-full wonder-full wonder-full wonder-full wonder-full wonder-full wonder-full full wonder-full wonder-full **wonder-full** wonder-full wonder-full wonder-full wonder-full wonder-full wonder-full wonder-full wonder-full wonder-full wonder-full wonder-full wonder-full wonder-full wonder-full wonder-full wonder-full wonder-full wonder-full **wonder**

# 1

## The Wonder of Wondering

∞

*Destiny is a mysterious thing, sometimes*
*enfolding a miracle in a leaky*
*basket of catastrophe.*

—FRANCISCO GOLDMAN[1]

You've entered the cinema and are very excited about seeing a great movie that has been touted by the media for
months and months. You are happy that none of your friends
nor the media have revealed the ending. In fact, at dinner last
night, you stopped someone from blurting it out as you put
your hands over your ears and started singing loudly. It got a
great laugh, and your friend got the point . . . he didn't reveal
the ending. You wanted to experience the story for yourself.
You didn't want the movie spoiled. Think about that. It would
*spoil* the movie if you knew the ending.

Wouldn't it be wonderful if we could think of the story of
our lives in just this way? We could allow ourselves to be the
observer of the greatest story ever told . . . at least to our-

selves. I WONDER what's going to happen. I WONDER! Strangely, as much as we worry about the uncertainty of the future, I believe that if someone could tell us in advance how things were going to turn out, we wouldn't want to hear it. Oh, yes, we love fortune-tellers to tell us that we will be rich, healthy, and find true love. It's always great to hear the good stuff, but I don't think we'd like to hear the "bad" stuff, and, of course, some "bad" stuff is likely to occur in all our lives.*

Suppose that I had the power to predict the future with absolute certainty, which, of course, I don't, and I presented you with the following chronicle of your life:

> You will be happily married at the age of twenty-eight.
> You will be divorced at the age of thirty-five.
> Your mother will die when you are thirty-seven.
> You will have a kidney operation when you are forty-two.
> You will have two children . . . a boy and a girl. The boy will be great. The girl will be a terror.
> You will remarry at the age of forty.
> You will have a great relationship with your new husband.
> Your husband will die at the age of seventy-three.
> You will die at the age of eighty-four.

And everything in between. If this were describing the events of your life, would you really want to know? Again, I

---

*As you will learn, there is no such thing as "bad" if we can find the learning and growth that come from it all.

don't think you would. I think your advance knowledge of the bad stuff, and there's always bad stuff, would make you a nervous wreck.

And how would knowing how things would turn out affect your decisions? For example, how would you approach your first marriage knowing it would end in divorce? Perhaps you would not have married in the first place. If you chose not to marry, perhaps you would have missed some wonderful and valuable experiences.

As I mentioned earlier, I married my first husband at the age of eighteen, and I was divorced at the age of thirty-four. Had I known before I married him that the marriage would definitely end in divorce, would I have married him? Probably not. Would I have missed many wonderful experiences and great learning? Absolutely. Even though we are now divorced, it was not *all* bad. I am not unhappy about the great times we had together, the great children we raised, and so many other things. And, very significantly, it was largely what I learned from my first marriage that helped me create the very loving and joyous second marriage that I'm in right now.

Isn't it better that we take things as they come . . . the good and the bad . . . and learn and grow as events happen? I believe that each moment, each day, each age, each experience brings with it its own challenge. And the trick is to learn to love the uncertainty of it all. I know that these are words, just words, that can't describe the pain in which some of us find ourselves at times. But if we can transfer the feeling of upset, even panic, about the future into the understanding that we can learn and grow from it all, we will have made great progress.

And, do we really want to ruin the challenge of it all . . . the surprise around the corner . . . the true adventure of "not-knowing"? If we can shift our uncertainty, our not-knowing, into an adventure, how wonderful that would be. Even if things go wrong, we would always be the seeker rather than the victim. "I wonder how this will all turn out." "I wonder what I am going to do about this." "I wonder what I will learn from this." The good news is that we can train ourselves to be adventurers instead of worriers. We can come to the realization that uncertainty is a very exciting thing. And when you think about it, if we really want to be happy, *what other choice do we have?* The unknown . . . the uncertain . . . defines so much of our lives. Do we want to be miserable or do we want to be excited about life? I suspect you prefer the latter.

For us to reach such an enviable way of being requires that we take a look at our present habits of being in this world and change what doesn't work for us. We need to develop healthier habits that give us peace of mind and make our lives more productive, loving, and fun. As many of you may already know from my earlier books and tapes, I am a lover of daily exercises to help us develop healthier habits, that is, exercises that help us move from the thinking of the Lower Self (that part of ourselves that is filled with insecurity, doubt, pain, and fear) to the thinking of the Higher Self (that part of ourselves that is filled with peace, confidence, power, and love). Trust me when I tell you that things always look better in the arena of the Higher Self. It is here that we find the power to embrace all the uncertainty in our lives.

You can make the exercises a lot more fun when you share them with a friend who wants to improve the quality of his or her life as much as you do. Mutual motivation is a very good thing. It really helps to have someone prod you along when you get lazy . . . and vice versa. It's a win-win situation for the both of you.

I'm sure you've found, as I have, that even though we know certain behaviors can really help us, we not only resist doing them, we actually forget to do them. That's because our Lower Self is stuck in its own habits and doesn't want to change. It really wants to have control. It does not want you moving up to the level of the Higher Self, where peace of mind can be found. It wants you to stay in the muck and mire of its negative thoughts.

I implore you . . . don't let it have its way! Make the commitment to stay the course that leads to the best of who you are. And here's the first exercise to get you started. Enjoy!

---

### THE "I WONDER" EXERCISE

---

This exercise is designed to help you create a "Wondering Life" instead of a "Hoping Life." Hoping can lead to a state of unhappiness if those very hopes are dashed.* It can create a fear of the uncertainty, even if those hopes are even-

---

*And, of course, this includes wishing, wanting, desiring, and any other such emotion that opens you up to disappointment, sadness, and upset in the future.

tually realized. It can blind us to valuable opportunities for growth.

Wondering, on the other hand, doesn't result in unhappiness, as there are no hopes to be shattered. And with the magic of wondering, fear of the uncertain is replaced by *curiosity*. Wonder can also open our eyes to valuable opportunities for growth. You can see why, when we substitute a Wondering Life for a Hoping Life, we have taken one important step toward embracing uncertainty.

What follows are three variations of the same theme. Any one of the three will help you in your goal of discovering the wonder of wondering. *Naturally, you will be better served by doing all three . . . over and over again!*

1. Find yourself a large blank sheet of paper and draw a line down the center. (All exercises of this type can, of course, be done on a computer.) On the left side, begin listing all of your hopes for the future. An example would be "I hope the party is a great success." Keep going until you can't think of any more. Don't stop there. Just keep thinking a little longer until a few more hopes pop into your mind. You will be surprised how many of them are stuffed into our heads and hearts. In fact, our lives are consciously or subconsciously filled with hopes for all kinds of things every moment of every day.

Once you've finished your list of hopes, it's then time to fill in the right side of your paper with sentences of wonder instead of hope. Let me illustrate . . .

| A HOPING LIFE | A WONDERING LIFE |
|---|---|
| I hope he'll call. | *I wonder if he'll call.* |
| I hope I lost some weight. | *I wonder if I lost any weight.* |
| I hope the bus comes soon. | *I wonder if the bus will come soon.* |
| I hope I get the job. | *I wonder if I'll get the job.* |
| I hope I have kids. | *I wonder if I'll have kids.* |
| I hope I have a happy marriage. | *I wonder if I'll have a happy marriage.* |
| I hope my blind date is handsome. | *I wonder what my date looks like.* |
| I hope my son does well in school. | *I wonder if my son will do well in school.* |
| I hope I get a raise. | *I wonder if I'll get a raise.* |
| I hope I am always healthy. | *I wonder if I'll always be healthy.* |

You will notice how the pressure about the future is relieved when we live in a wondering world. In the next chapter, we will take this a step further, but for now notice that, when you take away the hoping, wishing, wanting, and desiring, you are much more open to having it go either way, thereby being able to relax as the future unfolds. "I wonder how this story will end." It's the stuff from which good movies are made.

2. This variation of the "I Wonder" exercise asks you to take a look at your diary or daily planner and, on a separate piece of paper or on your computer, make a list of activities

that are coming up the following day. After each activity on the list, write, "I wonder how this will turn out." *There is no hoping, there is only wondering.* Then, at the end of each day, again, as if it were the end of a film, record how it actually did turn out.

It is common for us to make statements about approaching events such as, "I hope Tom and I will have a great dinner tonight." Again, this kind of statement inherently has the opportunity for disappointment since hopes are often shattered. The dinner may be lousy. And you are disappointed. When that sentence is changed to "I wonder how my dinner with Tom will turn out," you create an opportunity for a win-win situation. It may be good or it may be bad, but you have reduced the emotional investment that hoping usually brings. You have also increased your opportunity for adventure instead of judgment.

3. Another variation: Each morning as you wake up to face a new day, say to yourself,

"I wonder what will happen in my life today."

You do *not* say to yourself, "I really hope this happens" or "I really want this to happen." Then, at the end of the day, record what actually did happen in your life that day. You may want to place a sticker displaying the sentence, "I wonder what will happen in my life today," on your mirror, your refrigerator, or your desk just to remind you. How quickly we forget!

This is a very important step toward peace of mind. Instead of stating you want things to turn out a certain way, you are simply reporting how it all happened. You step out of yourself to become the observer. You take note of all the events that occur during the day as the reporter or the journalist. Yes, you may experience all manner of emotions throughout the day, as we all do—fear, love, joy, upset, anger, delight, and so on—but you are *the observer* of these emotions as well. When you become the observer, you are not trapped in the drama when times are bad and you can be appreciative when they are good.

Here is a shortened version of what it will look like . . .

*Morning*: I wonder what will happen in my life today . . .
*Evening*: This is what happened in my life today . . .

> I had a headache all morning. It put me in a bad
>   mood.
> I had a great lunch with Lydia. I really enjoy being
>   with her.
> My meeting with my boss didn't go well at all. I
>   think I better "feel the fear and do it anyway" and
>   get a new job. It's time!
> I saw the movie *Schindler's List*, and it was great. I
>   cried through the whole picture.
> Dinner with Bob was a bit tense. I *wonder* if he'll
>   call again.

Notice in this last item that you are not hoping he will call, you are wondering. Immediately you've taken the drama out of the experience. No hopes can be dashed. He'll call or he won't. ("I wonder how this movie will end.") Also notice that you didn't spend the day filled with hopes and expectations that can be dashed. You are simply the observer of the facts and your emotions.

I know we are told to always have hope. In a sense this is better than having no hope. It is better than feeling nothing will work out for you. "I bet I won't get the job." "I bet I won't be able to have kids." "I bet I won't have a happy marriage." "I bet my date is a jerk." And when you bet something will be lousy, you will usually ensure that it is. How depressing! Yes, hoping is better than pessimism. But, as I have tried to show you, even hoping has its downside. It can actually create an intense experience of suffering. It certainly keeps us from enjoying the present. Perhaps instead of the popular saying "Don't give up hope," we need to say, "Just learn from the huge adventure of it all."

Wondering neutralizes both hoping and pessimism. It allows us to handle better what life brings us. It helps us drop our need for control of the uncontrollable, thus setting us free. It cleans the slate for the future and relieves us of much anxiety. You can see why it's time to create a Wondering Life for ourselves instead of a Hoping Life. A Wondering Life is filled with . . . yes . . . wonder.

As I already told you, when I was young, I needed to know exactly what life was going to hand me. More and more I am learning to like the adventure of not-knowing. So I ask you to join me in calling forth the adventurer and the observer within yourself. Immediately a sense of peace will begin to stir in the depths of your being. Always remember . . .

Don't wish for it to happen.
Don't wish for it not to happen.
Just watch it happen.
Let the wonder of life unfold.

open your mind open your mind open your mind open your mind open your mind open your mind open your mind open your mind open your mind open your mind open your mind open your mind open your mind open your mind open your mind open your mind open your mind open your mind open your mind open your mind open your mind open your mind open your mind open your mind open your mind open your mind open your mind open your mind open your mind open your mind open your mind open your mind open your mind open your mind open your mind open your mind open your mind open your mind open your mind open your mind open your mind open your mind open your mind open your mind open your mind open your mind open your mind open your mind open your mind open your mind open your mind open your mind open your mind open your mind open your mind open your mind open your mind open your mind open your mind open your mind open your mind open your mind open your mind open your mind open your mind open your mind open your mind open your mind open your mind open your mind open your mind open your mind open your mind open your mind open your mind open your mind open your mind open your mind open your mind open your mind open your mind open your mind open your mind open your mind open your mind open your mind open your mind open your mind open your mind open your mind open your mind open your mind open your mind open your mind open your mind open your mind open your mind open your mind open your mind open your mind open your mind open your mind open your mind open your mind open your mind open your mind open your mind open your mind open your mind open your mind open your mind open your mind open your mind open your mind open your mind open your mind open your mind open your mind open your mind open

# 2

# The Power of Maybe . . .
# The Value of Doubt

∞

*The trouble with the world is that the stupid are*
*cocksure and the intelligent are full of doubt.*

—BERTRAND RUSSELL

I loved Sting's response when he was asked "What is the trait you deplore in others?" His answer was "Blind certainty."[1] Have you noticed that so many people in today's world have this trait of blind certainty? What makes this trait so lamentable is that with it goes an unyielding need to be right. Certainly this would have described me a number of years ago. In fact, as many of you already know, I consider myself a recovering know-it-all! I used to be so cocksure about everything . . . at times, to the point of obnoxiousness. I admit that, even now, I slip back into it once in a while, but more and more I am learning that . . .

I DON'T REALLY *KNOW* ANYTHING!

And neither does anyone else. The good news is that I have learned there is an incredible amount of freedom in that recognition. And there is more. Leo Tolstoy observed so long ago that . . .

The only thing that we can know is that we know nothing and that is the highest flight of human wisdom.[2]

So not only are we feeling a sense of freedom with our not-knowing mind, we are also feeling incredibly wise!

Yes, there are many advantages to cutting our very destructive attachment to knowing it all, to being right. Certainly letting go of blind certainty not only makes us less deplorable (à la Sting's observation), it also opens our eyes to the wonder which, as you have already learned, leads us to a great adventure in learning.

Gestalt therapist Barry Stevens tells us that the Jains in India have a word that means "to the best of my knowledge at this time." That word is "syat." Stevens says that they toss it into conversation frequently to remind others and themselves that is all that anyone has to go on.[3] When we toss in the word "syat," it states that perhaps there is no such thing as the truth, only "MAYBE" which means, "I think, but I'm not sure."

What we as human beings constantly forget is that we have mortal eyes. And while mortal eyes are truly a miracle, the reality is that they cannot see beyond the walls of a room. Ironically, when we close our eyes, our vision is a bit wider . . . but just a little bit. In the mind's eye, we can actually rise above the clouds. We can soar. We can imagine, picture, and pretend. But there is nothing in our human makeup that allows us to see what I love to call the Grand Design.

Elsewhere, I have described the Grand Design as the larger dimension, the larger plan of the Universe that is beyond our grasp as an ordinary mortal to see or understand. We can guess, ponder, and surmise, but we'll never "know." And anyone who says they do know makes their world much smaller and much more frightening than it need be.

We need only look around to see that the blind certainty that so many of us possess is responsible for creating tension and unrest in our lives instead of flow. In a world of discovery, instead of blind certainty, we can relax and let go of our need for things to be a certain way. This does not mean we stop taking action to create important changes in our lives and in our world, but it does mean that we let go of how we think it's *supposed* to be or how it *should* turn out. Again, we let go because we don't really know the Grand Design. When we drop our attachment to any outcome, we start feeling that all-important WONDER. We start feeling curious about how it will turn out. The emotional hold that attachment creates melts away, and we are free to engage with others in a more encompassing way. Life gets bigger and certainly easier.

So how do we get ourselves out of the habit of thinking with closed minds? And, truly, it is a habit. Obviously, when we are more comfortable with the great adventure of not-knowing, we are much better able to embrace the uncertainty that we are totally unable to avoid. I've come up with a few insights and exercises that have really helped me. Let me share them with you.

Over the years, I have come to the conclusion that MAYBE is a very powerful word. In the past, I would have thought that "powerful" would have described words such as . . .

LOVE

STRENGTH

TRUTH

I have now added the word . . .

MAYBE

I know you may be skeptical, so let me expand on the advantages of living in a MAYBE world, and there are many.

First, when you live in a MAYBE world, you are better able to control your upset and anger when others express opinions that differ from yours. In a MAYBE world, you realize that . . .

MAYBE I'M RIGHT, MAYBE I'M WRONG.

Or similarly . . .

MAYBE SHE'S RIGHT, MAYBE SHE'S WRONG.

There is much peace in this awesome awareness. Let me give you an example. Just before I started writing this chapter, the world watched a very contentious battle for the United States presidency. Passions raged on both sides of the political spectrum. To put it mildly, I watched my own temper flare on a number of occasions. When I reminded myself that I live in a MAYBE world, my upset with those in the opposing party, including a few of my friends, disappeared, and I was better able to hear what they were saying. While I never changed my mind about certain issues, I was able to open my mind and heart, and I learned a lot. I kept reminding myself that . . .

Maybe I'm right, maybe I'm wrong. Maybe they're right, maybe they're wrong. Nobody knows what the future holds. Nobody knows the Grand Design.

Having adopted this MAYBE attitude, I was able to flow with the political e-mails coming in from all over the place, the bemoaning of my like-minded friends at dinner, the politically slanted media, and so on. Again, this doesn't mean I necessarily changed my opinion on the issues of contention, but there was a level of understanding that had not been there before. I also realized that my vision is limited. I could be right, I could be wrong. Truth is only found in the Grand Design, which none of us can see. We always want to take action to create a better world, but we act with the understanding that maybe we're right, maybe we're wrong. Maybe their way is better or maybe our way is better. Only time will tell.

As you can see from the above example, when we have strong belief systems, we create boundaries in our lives. And our clue that we have strong belief systems is when we find ourselves continually defending something and needing to be right. Belief systems create boundaries in our learning, in our friendships, in our own capacity to discover new ways of thinking. These boundaries are created by an attachment to a way of thinking as opposed to freedom of thought. Freedom of thought allows the kind of discovery that expands our world and allows us to become the best that we can be.

There is no doubt that uncertainty, a "maybe I'm right, maybe I'm wrong" way of seeing the world, opens our minds to new learning. It gives us freedom to search for new ideas, new pathways, new directions. You may be surprised that some of the greatest advocates for uncertainty are scientists. For example, Richard Feynman, who received the Nobel prize for his work in quantum electrodynamics reported that he was never certain. In fact, he totally embraced uncertainty. He believed that when we take on the attitude of doubt, we open the channel for new inventions. To say that we are sure closes it. He said . . .

I feel a responsibility as a scientist who knows the great value of a satisfactory philosophy of ignorance, and the progress made possible by such a philosophy, progress which is the fruit of freedom of thought.[4]

Isn't that a wonderful phrase . . . *a satisfactory philosophy of ignorance?* Feynman learned over the years that progress is the fruit of freedom of thought that is created by a satisfactory philosophy of ignorance. Uncertainty allows freedom of thought; certainty cuts it off. He says we must be free to doubt.

Feynman isn't the only one to have reported a satisfactory philosophy of ignorance. Others throughout history have recognized the value of a state of doubt, of not-knowing. For example, the Dalai Lama is often heard to say three very valuable words, which are . . .

I DON'T KNOW.

Powerful words . . . I DON'T KNOW. Rick Fields pointed out that "not-knowing" in spiritual work is great wisdom. In fact, "don't-know mind" is the name for a method of meditation taught by the Korean Zen master Sahn Soen-Nim.[5] Not-knowing mind is clear mind.

One of my favorite Tai Ji masters, Chungliang Al Huang tells us that Tai Ji is a philosophy that starts with the basic not-knowing, the basic relaxation of giving in. Listen to the peace of those words . . . "the basic relaxation of giving in." Oh, if we could all relax into the wonderful world of not-knowing![6]

Another advantage to a MAYBE mind is that it helps to keep us from being disappointed. Is something good or bad? Maybe it is; maybe it isn't. This calls to mind the wonderful story about the farmer in old times who, one day, discovered his horse had wandered off into the forest. The neighbors said to him, "How unlucky to have your horse wander off." His response was "Maybe it is; maybe it isn't." Two days later, the horse came back, bringing with him another horse he befriended in the wild. The neighbors kept saying, "How lucky to have two horses." The farmer's response was "Maybe it is; maybe it isn't." A few days later, the farmer's son broke his leg trying to tame the new horse. Again, the neighbors chimed in, "How unlucky it is that your son broke his leg." And again, the farmer responded "Maybe it is; maybe it isn't." The following day, soldiers came to the farm to recruit the farmer's son. Because of his broken leg, he could not be recruited. Of course, the neighbors were amazed, and said, "How lucky it is that your son wasn't taken into the army." And you already know the farmer's response, "Maybe it is; maybe it isn't." You get the point . . . and hopefully a way to keep yourself from future disappointments.

Given all of the above, you can see how it makes us so much happier when we don't have the need to be right. I can tell you that when I was a total control freak (I'm only a partial one now), I was half-crazed in my need to be right. Finally, I learned that I can relax and be wrong sometimes and it's okay. In fact, it's more than okay . . . I can actually learn something new!

Trust me when I tell you that you will feel so much freer with the power of MAYBE. If we could all join together and derive what a leading management consultant, Richard Hallstein, calls a "collective comfort with our incompetence,"[7] we could all relax into a flow of joint efforts in creating a world where we come up with effective solutions in our own lives, our own communities and throughout the world.

I know it's hard to break our habit of needing to be right, but it's possible. Perhaps there should be another twelve-step program entitled "Control Freaks Anonymous." You would find a lot of people lining up to get in. In the meantime, how do we incorporate the power of MAYBE into our lives? Let's start with an obvious exercise.

## THE "MAYBE" EXERCISE

1) I love this exercise. My friends and family have been playing with it for a while and we are all having a lot of fun with it. We laugh a lot as we "correct" each other into the realization that it's a MAYBE world. It's a very simple exercise, and here is how it works.

From now on, until it becomes an automatic reaction in your head, end every one of your statements of certainty with the word MAYBE. For example . . .

I'll love my new job . . . . . . . . . . . . . . . . . . . . . *maybe.*
It's a perfect day for a walk . . . . . . . . . . . . . . *maybe.*
The president's speech was right on . . . . . . . . *maybe.*
Jane's new boyfriend is great . . . . . . . . . . . . . *maybe.*

Here's where a friend comes in handy once again. When you forget to add the critical word MAYBE to your statement, ask a friend to fill in for you. If you say, "A walk in the morning is good." She says, "Maybe." And vice versa. Of course you want to avoid doing this with friends who don't understand or who are too dogmatic to listen to reason . . . maybe. You get the point. Other words that you can throw into the conversation to help create a MAYBE world for yourself are . . .

IN MY OPINION
TO THE BEST OF MY KNOWLEDGE
AT THIS TIME, I BELIEVE
THE THINKING AT THIS TIME IS
I THINK

These are all forms of "syat," the Jain word I described above. As you can see, this takes certainty out of the picture and allows the far more desirable state of uncertainty in. It allows room for discovery, for openness, for adventure into the unknown.

2) Here is another variation of the MAYBE exercise. Let me give you an example of how it works. My friend's husband was an artist. He wasn't selling any paintings. This concerned my friend greatly because, even though she worked, it affected their finances, and, worse, it lowered her husband's self-esteem when he couldn't sell his art. She said, "I know they'll start selling soon." I said, "Or they won't." She looked a bit startled. I said, "What you need to realize is that you can find a way to make it work either way." She smiled, and said, "You're right. It will work either way." She realized in that instant that she was much better off letting go of the need for it to be a certain way. Maybe the Grand Design had something else for her husband to do. Who knows? Not me. Not you.

Some things are difficult to face, like the possible death of someone you love. A friend whose sister was diagnosed with breast cancer said to me, "I know she will beat it in the end." I reminded her, "Or she won't." I know you may think that this was a very cruel thing to say to someone who does not understand the value of doubt. And you may be right. But knowing my friend, I felt it would be an act of compassion. And it was.

I saw her visibly relax and surrender to the fact that she had no control. She said, "You're right. I may lose her. I know

I have to make every moment I have with her count. Thank you for reminding me to let go of the outcome." She also told me that her sister had commented to her what an incredible learning experience her bout with cancer had been and how it had brought her closer to everyone around her.

Again, no one knows the Grand Design and the meaning and purpose of it all. To ease our minds and hearts we must embrace the thought "It's all happening perfectly." And it truly is.

As you can see, the words "or it won't" become another form of MAYBE, such as the following:

I will have a great time tonight . . . . . . . . or I won't.
My children will grow up happy . . . . . . or they won't.
I know she will be okay in the end . . . . . or she won't.

Once again, you can see how the pressure is relieved, the expectations are erased, and opportunities for new learning emerge. Practice using these words as you go about your day. Even if, in the beginning, this concept is hard to accept in relationship to meaningful situations in your life, you will soon experience the relief that comes from letting go of the uncontrollable and focusing on the amazing power you have within to handle whatever happens in life.

And here's another very valuable exercise that will help you create a MAYBE world for yourself. It will come in handy in many situations in your life, whether they have to do with friends, "enemies," parents, children, or business associates.

## THE "BLENDING ENERGY" EXERCISE

This exercise could be considered an "aikido" approach to disagreement. Aikido is a form of the martial arts that has been translated to mean "the way of blending energy."[8] And certainly a blending of energy is what is most needed when conflict is in the air. A blending of energy also helps us promote the idea of a MAYBE world. Here is how it works.

Let's assume someone is coming at you with a strong verbal attack. Or maybe they are just strongly disagreeing with your opinion on a certain matter. You can easily move out of the line of attack and into a state of blended energy by simply saying something equivalent to . . .

"Tell me more. I'm interested to hear your views about this issue."

Magic. Do you feel the tension dissolve as an incoming energy of arrogance and self-righteousness is blindsided as you radiate an energy of openness and flow? In one fell swoop, you have set up the possibility for dialogue instead of disagreement. Powerful! And, in the end, you BOTH may learn something of value.

Of course, once you have made your Blending Energy statement, it is necessary for you to truly listen to what the other party is saying and continue to respond with an attitude of discovery. This is easier said than done. Why? *Because so many of us are totally controlled by our unfortunate need to be right!*

I suggest that you begin by memorizing a Blending

Energy phrase similar to the above that feels right for you. Then, when anyone comes at you in the form of an argument, simply embrace your opponent with an openness of head and heart. It is more likely than not that your adversary will soon calm down and be open to hearing your point of view as you listen to his. What will allow you to open your mind and heart more easily is to keep reaffirming that this is a MAYBE world. Maybe you're right; maybe you're wrong. Maybe he's right; maybe he's wrong. Maybe I'm right; maybe I'm wrong. Only time and circumstances will tell for sure . . . maybe.

You can use the Blending Energy exercise not only to deflect an attack, but also to stop yourself from attacking others. There are times in life when someone "presses your button." You know what I'm talking about. You can actually feel a physical reaction, a knotting up, when someone says something that rubs you the wrong way. Some of your friends, family, and acquaintances may actually know which buttons to press and how to press them to get an unfair advantage over you. I find children are masters at this. They know exactly the buttons to press in their parents to get a strong reaction! Again, pull out a Blending Energy statement such as . . .

"I'm curious as to why you see it that way?"

Just from my description you can see that as you move out of the way of conflict and into the centered state of flow, you break down the boundaries and convince yourself and your "opponent" to lay down the boxing gloves and create more understanding between the two of you.

Why does this exercise work so effectively? It has been shown that we all radiate an energy field that extends far beyond our physical body; that is, we don't end where our skin ends. Our aura, which some claim can be photographed by means of "kirlian" photography, demonstrates this phenomenon. But you don't need kirlian photography to see someone's energy field. It is easy to "feel" it. It is common for us to say about people in our lives, "It feels great to be around her," or "I feel uncomfortable around her." What we are "feeling" is the person's energy field. It can be positive or negative. I heard someone say recently that she wanted to take a shower every time she bumped into one of her acquaintances because she felt so tainted by her negativity! Yes, energy fields can be that toxic.

The good news is that we can change our energy field by changing our emotions. It stands to reason that when we are on the attack our aura radiates a very closed and negative energy. It sets up boundaries over which nobody can cross. Hardly the environment for blending energy! Nor is it the environment for growth and discovery . . . or making close friends.

The Blending Energy exercise sets the stage for you to be understanding, relative to the opinions of others. In the end, you may agree to disagree, but you do it with warmth and hopefully a hug. Just yesterday I encountered a man whose hostile views about certain issues that are important to me started to press my buttons. Immediately, I said to him, "Why do you feel that way?" He explained, and I listened. We continued to have a dialogue and in the end, I simply said, "I respect your opinion. I just see the world a little differently, and isn't it wonderful that we live in a country where we can each have our own views?" I then gave him a hug. He felt good and I felt good.

After hearing his viewpoint, I realized that if I walked in his shoes, I probably would be thinking as he does. I just happen to walk in different shoes. You will ultimately learn that in a MAYBE world, the need to be right greatly diminishes. Many of us are afflicted by this insidious cause of conflict to some extent, and it takes some work to get past it. We all need to learn how to lighten up. A lightness of the spirit allows us to move forward much more easily in life. In this case, it allows us to resolve conflict in a more enlightened manner.

As I have already suggested, it is not necessary for you to agree with the other person for the concept of Blending Energy to work. Resolving conflict isn't about who is right, rather it is about acknowledging and respecting different opinions. Resolving conflict requires only that you open up your heart, open your ears, and actually feel and hear what the other person is saying. You may incorporate some of the viewpoints of your opponent . . . or you may not. And vice versa. What is important is that you have left your ego at the door and opened yourself to learning and growth. A wonderful component of a MAYBE world.

I have found that as you slowly ease yourself into the Blending Energy technique, you will begin to let go, to learn, to listen, and to care. You will be willing to hear other points of view, *initially as a technique*, but later simply for the joy of discovery. You actually become interested in and open to the viewpoints of others, as opposed to being hostile and feeling angry. Trust me, a recovering know-it-all, when I tell you that the former feels so much better than the latter! As you let go of the attachments of the ego, you may even allow yourself to change your mind about certain of your belief systems. It takes a while to get into the flow, but it is definitely worth the effort. Life simply feels so much better when you are in a state of flow.

I can't leave this chapter without talking about the view-points of many experts today: Some are wise enough to real-ize that this is a MAYBE world. They have a "Richard Feynman" perspective. They believe, as Feynman did, that what we call scientific knowledge today is a body of state-ments of varying degrees of certainty. Some of these experts are very unsure. Some of them are nearly sure. But none are absolutely sure. They believe ALL scientific knowledge is, on some level, a guess. They know that a different "truth" may be found down the road.

On the other hand, there are experts who put their claims out into the world as absolute truths. Uncontestable. They "know" they are right. Have you ever heard two experts argu-ing on a talk show? One gives one interpretation of the situa-tion and one gives the opposite interpretation of the situation. If they are both "right," then why are they not in total agree-ment? Neither one has learned that this is a MAYBE world.

What is most "noticeable" about the two arguing experts is the negative energy created by their arrogance and self-righ-teousness. In its extreme, self-righteousness creates dogma-tism, rigidity, and intransigence. Hardly the traits of a wise person! We see this in so many religious and political extremists in today's world. When people are dogmatic, they insist that the rest of the world agree with them. And they denigrate those who don't. And that's how wars are started . . . big wars and little ones.

Over the years, I have encountered many "experts" who provide a perfect example of dogmatism. They KNOW every-thing. For example, when doing research for my book, *I'm Okay . . . You're a Brat,*[9] I was amazed by the "sureness" of many of the child-care experts giving advice to parents. "If you don't follow my advice, your children will grow up as ter-rorists!" Or something just as dire. I call these child-care experts the "guilt-gurus." To the unsuspecting, it sounds as if they really know what they are talking about.

The experts can guess and they can surmise, but if we just take a look around, we notice that a child can have the worst that life can offer and turn out wonderfully; and a child can have the best that life can offer and turn out horribly. Or, in the same family, one child can turn out to be great and the other horrible. Obviously, there are other factors entering into what I have coined the child's "Circle of Being."

And then there are the health claims. Some experts, for example, tell us that absolutely, for sure, we must eat a low-fat, high-carbohydrate diet in order to be healthy. Others tell us that absolutely, for sure, we must eat a high-fat, high-protein diet in order to be healthy.

What does this tell us? It tells us not to trust either one of them! It tells us that we must be suspicious of any expert who claims to know it all . . . who knows what is best for your health, who knows how to raise a healthy child, and so on. He or she is a pseudo-expert. A *real* expert of the best kind will tell you, "To the best of our knowledge at the present time, this is the information we have. Future research may prove us wrong."

Embracing the concept of a MAYBE world makes us healthily skeptical of experts who claim to know it all. The experts guess, but they don't know. Perhaps they actually believe their own rhetoric but, if they do, they certainly need to be sent back to school. They haven't learned, as Richard Feynman did, that the results of all scientific research have to be stated as guesses. They haven't learned that there are so many flaws in scientific research, and any other research, that to draw any final conclusions is irresponsible. This doesn't mean extrapolations aren't valuable; they are. But it is important that they are presented as guesses.

I recognize that some of you may be troubled by this realization. Many of us go to the experts hoping that they will have all the answers. (There's that hoping again!) "You mean they don't know for sure how to raise a healthy child, live a healthy life, secure all my money, and lose weight?" No, they don't. And it can be frightening to realize that they don't. But as you learn the concepts throughout this book, you will find ways to help you relax and put more trust in what "feels" right for you, your body, your family, and your life. As you learn to feel more comfortable in the not-knowing state of mind, you are much more open to investigation and discovery. And the wiser you become.

If you think about it, it is ironic that, by definition . . .

Know-it-alls close the door to knowing.

That's not very smart! As you practice the exercises in this chapter and throughout the book, you will become wiser than the pseudo-experts. And as you learn how to be okay with all the uncertainty and the not-knowing in this MAYBE world, you can look forward to all the new learning ahead of you. It's a magical world out there filled with so many opportunities for wondering . . . and discovery. Be grateful for it all.

let go let go let go let go let go let go let go let go let
go let go let go let go let go let go let go let go let go
let go let go let go let go let go let go **let go** let go let
go let go let go let go let go let go let go let go let go
let go let go let go let go let go let go let go let go let
go let go let go let go let go let go let go let go let go
let go let go let go let go let go let go let go let go let
go let go let go let go let go let go let go let go let go
let go let go let go let go let go let go let go let go let
go let go let go **let go** let go let go let go let go let go
let go let go let go let go let go let go let go let go let
go let go let go let go let go let go let go let go let go
let go let go let go let go let go let go let go let go let
go let go let go let go let go let go let go let go let go
let go let go let go let go let go let go let go let go let
go let go let go let go let go let go let go let go let go
let go let go let go let go let go let go let go let go let
go let go let go let go let go let go **let go** let go let go
let go let go let go let go let go let go let go let go let
go let go let go let go let go let go let go let go let go
let go let go let go let go let go let go let go let go let
go let go let go let go let go let go let go let go let go
let go let go let go let go let go let go let go let go let
go let go let go let go let go let go let go let go let go
let go let go let go let go let go let go let go let go let
go let go let go let go let go let go let go let go let go
let go let go let go let go let go let go let go let go let
go let go let go let go let go let go let go let go let go
let go let go **let go** let go let go let go let go let go let
go let go let go let go let go let go let go let go let go
let go let go let go let go let go let go let go **let go** let

# 3

## Freedom from Our Attachment to Unhappiness

∞

*When it starts to rain . . . let it!*

—U<small>NKNOWN</small>

---

*Dear Daddy,*
*I think I figured out what it is that I don't like about*
*roller coasters. I like to be in control of everything I*
*can, and when a machine is controlling where I'm*
*going, what I'm doing and when I stop and start, I get*
*scared. It's like when I'm talking on the phone, I get to*
*decide when I want to get off, but on a roller coaster, I*
*just have to stay on until it's over. That's what scares*
*me, that I'm not in control. I mean I don't care when it*
*stops and goes but thinking that I'm not in control is*
*scary. Anyways, I just thought I could share that with*
*you. I love you a lot and can't wait to talk to you about*
*this idea in the morning!*
*♥Always,*
*Jul*
*xoxoxo[1]*

I think if I had the choice of taking just one thing away from everyone reading this book, it would be expectations. And if I could add one thing, it would be trust. I'll talk more about trust later. Right now, let's focus on expectations. You may be wondering what I have against expectations, especially in a world where expectations are so ingrained in the fabric of our society. I'll tell you what I have against expectations:

Expectations, by definition, create an attachment, a yearning, a desire, a hope for something in the future to turn out a certain way. Of course, we have no control over what the future holds. Therefore, when we create expectations, *we automatically become our own worst enemy.* We sabotage ourselves as we set up a situation where first we "pre-worry" and then are disappointed if things don't turn out the way we want them to. And, if things do turn out the way we want them to, we don't have time for enjoyment because we are already "pre-worrying" about the next expectation we've created for ourselves. If this isn't self-sabotage, I don't know what is.

Expectations create within our being an intense need to control everything and everyone in the outside world . . . the weather, our boss, our children, our love life, and so on. As I've already discussed, not only is the future uncontrollable, most people and events in the outside world are also uncontrollable. Instead of letting go of trying to do the impossible, what do we do? *We try harder!* A little bit more self-sabotage, I'd say.

Expectations take away our peace of mind. We become control freaks as we obsess about the way it's "supposed to" be. As a "recovering control freak," I know whereof I speak!* Instead of doing our absolute best and then letting go, we lie awake at night thinking of things we could have done or should have done to make things turn out differently than they did. We have never learned that hindsight is useful to educate us, not upset us. When we can let go of how it is supposed to be, we can finally relax and be more peaceful with the way it is.

Expectations keep us from noticing and playing with exciting possibilities that always surround us. As long as we insist that things have to be a certain way, we limit our vision. When we let go of our expectations, we live with a greater sense of creativity, curiosity, and possibility. We understand that LIFE IS HUGE!

Expectations make us feel insecure. As we get lost in our fears that things may not turn out the way we want them to, we lose sight of our amazing capacity to make something wonderful out of all situations . . . even when they don't fit our picture of the way things are "supposed to" be. (I'll talk much more about this "amazing capacity" later.)

Expectations rule our emotions, our judgments, and sometimes, our actions. They carry with them disappointment, rigidity, anger, impatience, and obsession.

---

*Yes, not only am I a recovering know-it-all, I'm also a recovering control freak!

You notice that I haven't mentioned peace of mind, joy, fun, creativity, or spontaneity. That is because these wonderful feelings go with *a lack of expectations*. The irony is that while we think our expectations are giving us a measure of control, our expectations are really controlling us!

Need I go on? As you can see, expectations are not necessarily a good thing. Nor are they conducive to our ability to embrace all the inevitable uncertainty in our lives.

Now that you are aware of the damage that expectations can do, I trust that you will want to detach from your own expectations as quickly as possible. I ask you, why be disappointed, rigid, angry, impatient, and obsessive when you could be calm, joyful, happy, creative, and spontaneous?

As you learned in an earlier chapter, "Not-knowing" is the path of wisdom. Here you are learning that . . . "Non-attachment" is the path of a peaceful mind. Non-attachment allows us to look at all possibilities for the future with what health expert, Bernard Jensen, called a "relaxed consciousness."[2] A relaxed consciousness . . . what a freeing image. And Gestalt therapist, Barry Stevens, talked about "un-setting" our hearts. She said . . .

When I un-set my heart upon something I breathe more deeply and feel more free. Narrow escape.[3]

Another of my favorite images for feeling free is "wearing this world as a loose garment." A loose garment gives us room to move, to be comfortable, to flow, to not take it all quite so seriously. And martial arts expert Tom Crum used the image of "dancing on a shifting carpet." He says . . .

> Instead of seeing the rug being pulled out from under us, we can learn to dance on a shifting carpet.[4]

Put these images together and you can feel yourself breathing a sigh of relief . . .

> I relax my consciousness. I un-set my heart. I wear the world as a loose garment. I learn to dance with grace on the constantly shifting carpet.

These, of course, are great affirmations for creating a peaceful body and a peaceful mind.

Understand that an expectation is a fantasy, an illusion. It has no basis in reality. We make pictures in our mind and then are upset when reality steps in. When you're feeling lousy about something happening in your life or in the world, it isn't about the "something happening" that is the problem, it's your inability to let go of the expectation of how it's supposed to be.

Buddhism tells us that while pain is a natural part of every life, we can end the suffering by letting go of our need for things to be a certain way. This is the ultimate in wisdom and freedom. Most problems aren't problems. It's only our attachment to things being other than they are that makes them problems. Attachment brings suffering. Once we drop the attachment, the suffering falls away.

Of course, we may have "preferences" in life; but as long as they remain preferences and not attachments, life flows. It becomes, "Oh, well . . . let's move on," instead of "This is terrible . . . my life is ruined." Yes, life sometimes is difficult—sometimes very, very, very difficult—but extra pain is certainly created by our attachment to specific outcomes. It seems to me that . . .

The prime cause of our suffering is our wanting things to be different than they are!

Let me give you a few examples of how expectations mess us up and how non-attachment to outcomes can bring us a greater sense of peace.

1. You arrive at the airport and discover that your plane will be leaving three hours later than scheduled. Your expectation was that the plane would leave on time. You are upset. Your heart starts racing. You are annoyed with the airline employees (as if the people behind the counter created the problem with the plane's engine!). You start lamenting that you are being robbed of three hours of your valuable vacation time. Poor me. Victim! Victim! Victim! If you could unset your heart, loosen up, and detach from the way "it's supposed to be," you could notice the amazing opportunities for "vacationing" in the airport as you wait. How often do we find three hours to read, to people-watch, to strike up conversations with others, to eat, to drink, to shop, and to hang out with a sense of freedom? These times are rare in our every-

day lives. And we can make them something wonderful when they happen . . . that is, if we let go of our expectation that the plane has to leave at a certain time. It's just all part of the adventure.

2. You have an expectation, a hope, a desire to get a certain job. Someone else is hired. What do you feel? Disappointment, the insecurity that maybe you are not good enough for the job, fear that there won't be any other jobs out there, and so on. Let's assume you had decided beforehand to un-set your heart, letting go of your attachment to getting the job. You figured that if the job was meant to be yours, it would be. If it wasn't, there would be something else out there or maybe you were meant to be going in another direction. Therefore, if you get it, that's great. If you don't get it, that's also great. To increase your understanding, you might decide to learn as much as you could as to why you didn't get the job, (if you didn't), but you don't allow it to take away your happiness.

3. You have an expectation that your marriage will last "forever." In truth, it will or it won't! In *Opening Our Hearts to Men*, I tell the story of Maxine, who felt totally betrayed and devastated when her husband of twenty-three years left her for another woman. Because of her expectations of forever, her reaction to the situation was fairly predictable and understandable. "That creep! I gave him the best years of my life and look what he did to me!" Victim! Victim! Victim! I know that such an experience is very painful to deal with. But an expectation about "forever" makes it much worse. Maxine never understood that when her husband originally said "for-

ever," he probably meant it, but sometimes human beings change their minds. We cannot trust "forever." But we can learn to trust ourselves to handle whatever happens in our lives in a powerful and loving way. To quote myself (which I often do!) . . .

If we can perceive our mates as human beings who won't always follow our script, we can keep an open heart. If we have fairy tale expectations, our hearts can be easily broken and it is hard to "fix" them again.[5]

I joke that I always love my husband, Mark, to tell me he will love me forever, but I rest a little easier knowing I don't have to hold him to it! "Forever" was the theme of my first marriage. Obviously that didn't work. It didn't work for Mark's first marriage either. So what is the theme we've created for this marriage? We don't think about forever. We think about today. And, whenever we are together, we focus on how we can validate, respect, appreciate, and care for one another. And what a wonderful love we have created. When you think a love will last forever, you tend to forget to focus on the now . . . and that is how love dies. When you focus on acting lovingly today, love tends to grow and grow. At least that's how it's been for us.

Now that you see there are ways to live our lives other than in a state of expectation, you will notice that to give up our expectations is a very difficult thing to do. The word "habit" comes to mind, and habits are hard to break. We automatically create expectations that we hang on to, and we forget to let go. Of course, when we hang on to anything, we are stuck!

Here are two valuable exercises designed to help you let go. If you can make them part of your everyday routine, you will increasingly notice a blessed state of peace creeping into your previously troubled mind.

---

## THE "SCISSORS IN THE MIND" EXERCISE

I love using this exercise and I've given you a variation of it in other contexts. Here I am using it to deal with our expectations. As I have just explained, expectations lead us into a state of attachment. What we now need to do is "cut the cord" and feel the freedom of non-attachment. In so doing, we relax the grasping hand of our fear and neediness. I recently heard actress Drew Barrymore say in an interview that, once a film is complete, she doesn't worry about it anymore. She lets go of expectations because, if she didn't, then she would be unhappy. Wise woman! In effect, she is cutting the cord to her expectations.

How do we cut the cord? Obviously, the cord that needs to be cut is in our minds. Therefore, the moment an expectation in the form of a hope, desire, or wish of any kind comes into your head, you can shut your eyes and in your mind's eye, create an image of yourself actually tied to that expectation. As long as you are tied, you are not free. Then, in your mind's eye, see yourself cutting that connection. Here are two ways of using this valuable exercise.

1. Using the same Hoping List I created in Chapter 1, let me demonstrate the Scissors in the Mind exercise.

*I hope he'll call.*

You met a wonderful man at a party last night. As you are sitting at your desk, the thought "Why hasn't he called?" comes into mind. This is the logical sentence that emanates from the hope that he will call. You start to brood, obsess, and it is difficult to focus on the present. It's at this point that you shut your eyes and, in your mind's eye, imagine yourself cutting the imaginary cord that attaches you to this thought. Then you take a deep breath and imagine this hope floating off into the distance. The reality is that he'll call or he won't! You have no control over his actions. And your mind is now free to think more nourishing thoughts, for example . . .

> "This man is not my life. While I would enjoy seeing him again, I know I have the power to create a great life whether he calls or not. All is well."

When you cut the cord, you are free. When you fill yourself with nourishing thoughts, you are empowered. (Of course, being rather brazen in my dating days, I would be the one to pick up the phone and call him! But that's another story.)

*I hope I get the job.*

As in the above example, in your mind's eye, cut the cord to your hope of getting the job and breathe a sigh of relief. Feed yourself some nourishing thoughts:

> "If I don't get the job, it wasn't for me. There are many other jobs out there and my search will teach me very valuable lessons."

*I hope I have kids.*
In your mind's eye, cut the cord to the desire to have kids and breathe a sigh of relief. Feed yourself some nourishing thoughts:

> "Whether I have kids or not, there are so many ways of putting love into this world. Either way, I'll create a great life for myself and those around me."

*I hope I have a happy marriage.*
In your mind's eye, cut the cord to your desire that your marriage turns out a certain way, and breathe a sigh of relief. Feed yourself some nourishing thoughts:

> "I will put love and caring into my marriage and trust that whatever happens will be for my highest good and that of my spouse. If my marriage is happy, all is well. If my marriage is not happy, all is well. While I know that pain is part of the process, I also know that I will make appropriate adjustments and get to the other side of the pain while learning and growing all the way."

*I hope my blind date is handsome.*
In your mind's eye, cut the cord to how your blind date "should" look and breathe a sigh of relief. Feed yourself some nourishing thoughts:

> "I notice that I am focusing too much on outer qualities and not inner qualities. I will do my best to focus on what I like about him and try to make him

feel great as a human being whether he's cute or not."

*I hope I get a raise.*
In your mind's eye, cut the cord to your getting the raise and breathe a sigh of relief. Feed yourself some nourishing thoughts:

> "If I get the raise, that's great. If I don't get the raise, it's okay. I will manage somehow. It might be my cue to look at other options that are out there."

*I hope I am always healthy.*
In your mind's eye, cut the cord to your desire to always be healthy and breathe a sigh of relief. Feed yourself some nourishing thoughts:

> "Few of us escape some manner of physical problems as we age. I will do my best to stay healthy and trust that I will deal beautifully with any illness that happens to come my way."

*I hope my son does well in school.*
In your mind's eye, cut the cord to your son's experience of school and breathe a sigh of relief. Feed yourself some nourishing thoughts:

> "I have little control over how my son does in school. I will always be there to guide him, but I have to let go of thinking I can control how he does in school. Who

knows what experiences my son needs to go through in his journey through life? I certainly don't. I let go and I trust that all is happening for my highest good and that of my son."

Remember that in each case:

a) The cord is being cut to a future expectation,
b) Breathing a sigh of relief relaxes our consciousness and allows us to un-set our hearts and free ourselves from futile worry;
c) Nourishing thoughts help us realize that we will handle all that happens in our lives in a life-affirming way.

Now that you understand what is happening in this exercise, let's bring it closer to home. First, think about your own life and make a list of some expectations in the form of actual hopes, desires, and wishes that you are harboring right now. These expectations may be about your child's report card, your dinner party, your car's performance, your family's health, your love life, money, politics, the state of the world, and whatever else is of concern for you today from the smallest to the largest of issues.

Then going down the list, one by one,

a) Close your eyes . . .
b) Take out those imaginary scissors in the mind, and cut the cord to that expectation . . .

c) Imagine your expectation drifting off into the air until it is gone. Don't forget to breathe a sigh of relief.

d) Feed yourself some nourishing thoughts that put the situation into a healthier perspective.

Practice doing this over and over again. Soon you will be able to let your thoughts about future events drift off into space where they belong as you fill yourself with life-affirming messages of power, love and fulfillment.

2) Another variation of the Scissors in the Mind exercise can truly help you create a peaceful day. Anytime you are feeling upset, ask yourself,

"What am I holding on to that is causing this upset?"

It is often the case that whenever you are angry, upset, disappointed, self-centered, scared, jealous, or greedy, the likelihood is that you are attached to something. The key is to break the attachment. The minute you discover what is upsetting you, close your eyes, pick up those imaginary scissors, cut the cord to the expectation behind the upset, and breathe a sigh of relief as you watch it drift off into oblivion. Then feed yourself some nourishing thoughts.

You may have already learned from past experiences, that in the middle of your upset, when you most need to use a valuable tool, you totally forget that the tool is there to be used! Does that sound familiar? It is necessary therefore to create reminders. In this case, a reminder is easy. And that is . . .

Keep a pair of large scissors as a permanent feature on your desk or anywhere else you can see it to remind you to cut the cord.

Of course, *you don't want to put a scissors in the reach of small children,* but you can always find a safe place to put those scissors as a reminder to cut the cord to unhappiness.

I have used the Scissors in the Mind exercise to let go of many issues in my life. And the more I practice this exercise, my attachment to needing things to be a certain way has diminished to a very noticeable degree. Amazing. And, yes, I do keep a pair of real scissors on my desk to remind me. At times, I, too, forget! But less and less as time goes by.

---

## THE "I'LL WORRY TOMORROW" EXERCISE

---

The attempt to control the future and the demand to be in charge of everything in our lives sentences us to a daily existence obsessed with life-numbing worry. Many of us have attained the dubious title of "professional worrier." It seems as though it is our job to worry! Does the following example bear any resemblance to the way you think?

You are going on a long-awaited vacation. Your joy is marred by the multitude of things you are choosing to worry about . . . your computer being stolen, getting sick in unfamiliar territory, the plane being late, the hotel room being horrible, and whatever else you can think of that would destroy the experience of your trip. Sometimes it feels better just to stay home! Oh, if we could only think of it as a wonderful adventure . . . no matter what happens!

Even if things are going terrifically well, the mind of a professional worrier can always find something to worry about. For example, you have finally finished a project you've been working on for a long time. For one brief moment in time, you are happy. And then the worrying mind clicks in. "What if no other projects come to me?" "What if my clients don't like my work?" "What happens if I don't make enough money to cover my bills?" What if, what if, what if?

Another example: Your child finally makes the team. You have been worrying about it for weeks. You didn't want him to be disappointed. There is that one moment in time when you are happy he made the team. And then the worry kicks in. "What if he gets hurt?" "What if he is teased by other team members?" "What if his schoolwork suffers because of his daily practice?" What if, what if, what if?

As you can see, professional worriers limit themselves to very brief moments of happiness. This is because thoughts of potential future disaster immediately step in to take away the good feelings. It is a given that, when they have nothing to worry about, professional worriers invariably create something to worry about. To end this madness, we need to find a way to turn the worry off. The I'll Worry Tomorrow exercise can be the very thing we need to turn the worry off.

I have used this exercise very effectively for many situations in my life. It came to me as I was sitting at my desk worrying about the sale of our house. We wanted something smaller and the real estate market was good. My mind was driving me crazy with thoughts such as, "Where will we go when the house actually sells?" "Will we find another house that is just as satisfying as this one?" "Will we be able to sell our house at the price we want to get for it?" "Maybe no one will want it?" I laughed as I realized that *I was worried that the house would sell . . . and I was also worried that the house wouldn't sell!* Talk about creating a lose-lose situation in your mind!

I finally said to myself . . .

"I won't worry about anything today. I'll worry about it tomorrow."

And it worked! I felt my heart lighten. I felt worry-free for the entire day. And it has continued to work. Little by little, I am learning to repeat this simple thought about everything that tends to cause me worry . . . health, money, the happiness of my children, and so on.

We are often told not to put anything off until tomorrow if it can be done today. We now have at least one big exception to that rule . . . WORRY. I give you permission, just in case you feel you need it, to put off all your worry until tomorrow. It goes like this . . .

*Monday . . . repeat over and over again:*
"I won't worry about anything today. I'll worry about it tomorrow."

*Tuesday . . . repeat over and over again:*
"I won't worry about anything today. I'll worry about it tomorrow."
*Wednesday . . . repeat over and over again:*
"I won't worry about anything today. I'll worry about it tomorrow."
*Thursday . . . repeat over and over again:*
"I won't worry about anything today. I'll worry about it tomorrow."
*Friday . . . repeat over and over again:*
"I won't worry about anything today. I'll worry about it tomorrow."
*Saturday . . . repeat over and over again:*
"I won't worry about anything today. I'll worry about it tomorrow."
*Sunday . . . repeat over and over again:*
"I won't worry about anything today. I'll worry about it tomorrow."

Amazing! Seven worry-free days! And the last time I looked, there are only seven days of the week. If you do this for every week of your life, you have created a worry-free life. I know that this sounds very simplistic, but once you get the hang of it, you will find your life being dramatically uplifted since nothing will be able to pull you down . . . until tomorrow, which, of course, never comes.

It is important to understand that I am not saying that you should put off taking action TODAY to handle something that needs to be handled. *It just means you are not to worry about the outcome.* Taking action without worry ensures a clearer mind that allows you to get things done intelligently instead of emotionally. Taking action without worry allows you to do the very best that you can . . . whether it has to do with planning a party, raising children, or running a company. While many emotions improve the quality of our lives, others can sometimes get in the way. And worry is one of those emotions that too often gets in the way.

Let me illustrate: You are planning a party for your friends. In terms of action to take, this is what it looks like in both the "attachment" mode and "non-attachment" mode:

| ACTIONS TO TAKE WHEN ATTACHED TO OUTCOME | ACTIONS TO TAKE WHEN NON-ATTACHED TO OUTCOME |
| --- | --- |
| Create an invitation list | *Create an invitation list* |
| Create the invitations | *Create the invitations* |
| Mail the invitations | *Mail the invitations* |
| Buy the food | *Buy the food* |
| Buy the flowers | *Buy the flowers* |
| Cook the food | *Cook the food* |
| Pick an outfit to wear | *Pick an outfit to wear* |
| And so on. . . . . . . . . . . | *And so on. . . . . . . . . .* |

"Susan, the lists are exactly the same!" Yes, the actions in the "attached" and "non-attached" mode are usually the same or very similar. *The critical difference is how you experience it all.* If you are attached to the outcome . . .

You are nervous.

You are not enjoying the process.

You are experiencing and radiating tension.

If the party turns out well, you breathe a sigh of relief *when it's over* instead of enjoying it as it was happening. Why? Because you are happy that the tension is finally over! If the party turns out badly, you suffer with recriminations that you should have done it differently or you are angry at whoever or whatever may have "messed it up."

On the other hand, if you are not attached to the outcome and are in the present moment . . .

You are happy and excited.

You are enjoying the process.

You are experiencing and radiating love.

If the party turns out well, you are happy that people had a great time. If the party doesn't turn out well, you understand that you did your best and you can't control how other people interact or don't interact. You just keep sending loving energy to all who were there.

My guess is, the more relaxed you are relative to the outcome, the better the outcome will be. Your presence at the party will be more loving and flowing, and this positive energy is radiated out to everyone who is there. As a result, your guests will also be more loving and flowing. And you will have a wonderful time. Remember that the only thing you take in is what you relax to. Instead of being rigid and putting up a barrier to every possibility of nourishment, you are opening yourself up to be fed. In this way, you will have a much more joyous time at the party.

In all things, I suggest you create your goals. Do your best, Enjoy the work. Then let go of the outcome. When attached to outcomes, by definition, we are attached to unhappiness. As hard as we try, as fast as we go, we can never feel the security of being in control of the outside world. When we break our attachment to our expectations of control, we become happier people. If you knew you could find happiness in whatever state you found yourself—ill health or good health, rich or poor, in a great relationship or not, and so on—then your worry about the uncertainty in your life would be greatly diminished.

I know that releasing our expectations doesn't come easily in the beginning. In fact, sometimes when the chain is cut giving us the freedom to fly, we are terrified. While letting go offers the essence of security, it feels like we are giving up security. But, little by little, with practice, we come to the realization that . . .

When we finally are able to let go of the need for control, for the first time, we are truly in control.

So begin taking those little or big steps to help your mind learn how to let go. When you let go, your ability to embrace uncertainty will increase dramatically while your attachment to unhappiness will decrease dramatically. Hallelujah!

listen to the whispers listen to the whispers listen
to the whispers listen to the whispers listen to the
whispers listen to the whispers listen to the whispers
listen to the whispers listen to the whispers listen
to the whispers listen to the whispers listen to the
whispers listen to the whispers listen to the whispers
listen to the whispers **listen to the whispers** listen
to the whispers listen to the whispers listen to the
whispers listen to the whispers listen to the whispers
listen to the whispers listen to the whispers listen
to the whispers listen to the whispers listen to the
whispers listen to the whispers listen to the whispers
listen to the whispers listen to the whispers listen
to the whispers listen to the whispers listen to the
whispers listen to the whispers listen to the whispers
listen to the whispers listen to the whispers listen
to the whispers listen to the whispers listen to the
whispers listen to the whispers listen to the whispers
**listen to the whispers** listen to the whispers listen
to the whispers listen to the whispers listen to the
whispers listen to the whispers listen to the whispers
listen to the whispers listen to the whispers listen
to the whispers listen to the whispers listen to the
whispers listen to the whispers listen to the whispers
listen to the whispers listen to the whispers listen
to the whispers listen to the whispers listen to the
whispers listen to the whispers listen to the whispers
listen to the whispers listen to the whispers listen
to the whispers listen to the whispers listen to the
whispers listen to the whispers listen to the whispers
listen to the whispers **listen to the whispers** listen to

# 4

## Increasing the Odds

∞

*Logic is death to that part of you that is*
*the miracle maker.*

—STUART WILDE[1]

Yes, the future is uncertain. No doubt about it. And, as you learned in the last chapter, if you want to embrace the uncertainty, instead of being intimidated by it, you obviously have to learn how to let go of your expectations about how it all should turn out. No doubt about that either.

But what if there was a way to increase the odds that you are traveling in the right direction for your highest good? Shouldn't that way be explored? Of course, it should be. And, not to keep you in suspense one second longer, I'm talking about the fascinating world of intuition. I've briefly introduced you to this world in my earlier books, but now it is time to look at it more fully, as it is such a powerful tool in helping you make the uncertainty in your life more manageable and definitely more rewarding.

What exactly is intuition? As far as I can tell, no one really knows. People may guess, but they don't really know. Nor do they know how our intuitive sense gets its astounding wisdom. But there is no doubt that intuition is an incredibly powerful and under-utilized part of ourselves that is able to "see" things that our eyes cannot see and to "know" things that our thinking mind cannot know. In fact, it is only when we can get out of our thinking mind that we can use our intuitive mind to our greatest advantage.

Intuition is often talked about as a sixth sense, a hunch, ESP, insight, clairvoyance, telepathy, and the like. Many believe that the intuitive mind contains information that simply has been collected, consciously or unconsciously, and stored subliminally by the individual to be brought into consciousness at an appropriate time. But others, including me, believe it is something even more cosmic than that. For example, Frances Vaughan believes that intuition also includes "the infinite reservoir of the collective or universal unconscious, in which individual separateness and ego boundaries are transcended."[2] That's cosmic, indeed!

While not understanding the miraculous quality of intuition, we can envision it as an inner wisdom that has an inside "scoop" on what is happening in the outer world. It acts like a scout who has gone ahead, has seen the future, and can come back and tell us where to go. As a result, intuition can be a powerful means of protection. It can also lead us to where we need to go for a richer, fuller, more meaningful and exciting life.

If we want to get Spiritual about it, as I love to do, we can see it as our Higher Self connecting with a Higher Power and creating a Spiritual Intelligence, an incredible inner wisdom that can guide us in all areas of our lives. It is our connection to the Grand Design . . . that special plan that life has in store for us. It has a very wide reach to be sure!

Let me give you a stunning example of the power of the intuitive mind. In her fascinating book, *Awakening Intuition*, Dr. Mona Lisa Schulz, tells this story . . .

"We were having trouble with a study in which we were attempting to create artificial gonorrhea cells, or liposomes. No matter what we did, the cells would repeatedly leak like sieves. My supervisor was annoyed and impatient. One day he loomed over my lab bench, the veins bulging at his temples. Punching his finger at me, he demanded, 'What are you going to do about this?'

"I looked up at him. 'We'll try alpha-glucosidase!' I blurted—wondering even as I spoke what on earth alpha-glucosidase was, what it did, and, above all, where this wild idea had popped into my head from!

"My boss clearly wondered, too. He glared at me skeptically. 'What will that do?' he demanded. 'Where did you get that idea?'

"I asked him to leave me alone for a while, because I needed to take some time to write up a detailed experimental design that would fully address his questions and many others that would eventually come up. I went straight to the library and looked up alpha-glucosidase. After consulting several reference texts, I figured out how this enzyme might be used to design an artificial gonorrhea cell that wouldn't leak. I tried it in the lab, and it worked! Later that year, I presented a paper on the experiment at a scientific conference.[3]

This amazing event sent Schulz on a journey of discovery. She wondered what was going on in this Universe that would allow her to come up with the name of an enzyme she had never heard of, at the precise moment when she could receive and make use of it. She began investigating and learning to trust this powerful vehicle for entering into the world of the collective unconscious.

What does following our intuition feel like? Let me tell you how it feels to me. When I remove myself from my rational mind and tune in to my intuitive mind, it feels as though I am being led, instead of groping in the dark. It feels as though my choice is safe, even though it may seem like an illogical choice. It feels exciting, rather than frightening. It feels right instead of wrong. All of this, without knowing exactly why my choice is a good choice. It is a feeling that is not governed by my analytical mind; in fact, it may be at odds with my analytical mind. Certainly this is how it all felt in the following example from my own life. Some of you may have heard this story before, but I can't talk about intuition and not mention it. I think you will agree that it is an astounding story!

For about nine years, I had been the executive director of a wonderful health facility for the poor in New York City called the Floating Hospital.[4] One day, I was sitting at my desk, when the thought "Go to the New School for Social Research" came into my head. Where that thought came from, I haven't a clue. But since I was practicing the art of following directions from my intuitive mind, I decided to go, even though I had no idea why I was going. Or, for that matter, where I was going. (I had never been to the New School.) Since I was a "workshop addict" at the time, I figured they must be giving a great workshop I would enjoy taking.

When the cab delivered me to the front door of my mysterious destination, I was "led" by my intuition to the Human Relations Center. The receptionist wasn't at her desk and I found myself face-to-face with the head of the department, Ruth Van Doren. She asked if she could help me. And what came out of my mouth was a shock to me . . . I blurted out that I was there to teach a course on fear. This also came as a shock to Ruth Van Doren! With a look of astonishment on her face, she told me she had been searching for someone to teach a course about fear, she hadn't found a teacher yet, today was her deadline, and she had to leave in fifteen minutes. You can understand why I felt as if I had just entered the Twilight Zone! Within the next twelve minutes, I had written my course description, it was placed on the receptionist's desk with a note to include it in the course catalog, and Ruth Van Doren ran off to catch her bus. And what did I name the course? You guessed it . . . *Feel the Fear and Do It Anyway!*

Teaching that thirteen-week course changed my life. It was as though a mysterious door had opened up and showed me the way to a whole new career in teaching and writing books. While I loved my job at the Floating Hospital, my new career ultimately allowed me to spread my wings and touch people all over the world. Obviously, there was a bigger plan for my life than my rational mind was capable of imagining . . . but my intuitive mind was certainly tuned in! And I am thankful that I listened to what it was telling me, even though, at the time, it made no sense whatsoever.

As I stated above, there are many experts who close their minds to the broader and wider definition of intuition. They insist that intuition is just prior knowledge we acquired, consciously or unconsciously, that we simply have forgotten. Let's analyze my experience.

1. The New School was a place I had never been. I didn't even know where it was.
2. If I was going to present a course on fear or anything else, I would have gone to one of my alma maters—Hunter College or Columbia University.
3. I knew nothing about the New School and had never even seen one of their catalogs. Therefore I couldn't have known there was a Human Relations Center or what kind of courses it offered.
4. I couldn't have known that they needed someone to teach a course about fear. Nor could I have known that it was the last day to put the course in their catalog.

And I could go on and on with the astounding details. How did this "miracle of circumstances" happen? Where did the message, "Go to the New School," come from at that particular moment in time? I can't answer with certainty, but one thing I am certain about is that this was not "just prior knowledge forgotten." Sorry about that, you experts with the closed minds!

"Radio waves" come to mind. It was as though Ruth Van Doren was subliminally sending out a radio-like message into the Universe announcing that she was in need of someone to teach a class on fear. Unconsciously, my antennae were up, I was tuned in to her signal, and I heard the message. And, because I acted on this intuitive message, we were united in a mutual "purpose." So I like to imagine that the intuitive mind is hooked up to Universal radio waves, that is, Universal awareness.

Perhaps, this is not such a far-out interpretation. Enlightened experts in the field of physics, for example, are convinced more and more that we don't end where our skin ends. And "Do we end at all?" is the real question. It is possible that we are all an important part of the energy that encompasses the entire Universe. And, thankfully, we can all tune into this wonderful energy.

You may be skeptical about such an interpretation of intuition. But the good news is that, despite what you personally believe intuition to be, you can develop your own ability to better use it as a guide to a more meaningful future. It is interesting that the left brain is considered to be the home of the rational mind; the right brain is the home of the intuitive mind. Think back. Did anyone ever teach you how to develop your right brain function? Probably not. School, as we know it, is the place where we learn about the rational world of the five senses. It is not a place where we learn about the sixth sense, the world beyond the rational mind. You can understand how much richer our lives could be if we were educated to use both our right brain and left brain functions. We would then have logic combined with miracles. What an incredible combination!

The rest of this chapter is devoted to showing you how to better tune in to the world of intuition . . . and what an amazing world it is.

## THE "TUNING IN TO THE WORLD" EXERCISE

This mini-course on intuition comprises many components to play with and explore. Keep reviewing them, playing with them, opening up to them, and experimenting with them. Little by little, you will become aware of the awesome power of your own intuitive abilities.

1) *Focus on Your Highest Good:* Notice that in the opening paragraph of this chapter I didn't say that your intuition will lead you where your conscious mind thinks it should go. I said that your intuition will lead you to what is for your highest good. There is a big difference. Understand that the conscious mind is wonderful and very necessary, but it is very limited. It doesn't have BIG vision, GRAND vision, TALL vision, DEEP vision, nor does it have the ULTIMATE vision that only an understanding of the Grand Design provides. And, while it is beyond our ability to comprehend, our intuition definitely seems to have an understanding of the Grand Design.

2) *Quiet the Mind:* One way of raising the odds that you will find a satisfying solution to any problem is to stop thinking so hard and allow yourself to "know" what to do in any situation. Don't think . . . just know. Tune in to the Grand Design. I love Deepak Chopra's poetic observation that . . .

The cosmic psyche whispers to us softly in the gap between our thoughts.[5]

It is fascinating to think that we can learn more about the Universe "between our thoughts" rather than actually "from our thoughts."

Many of the tools I have discussed in prior books are very effective in helping to quiet the mind. I suggest you explore these tools which include meditation, Tai Ji, prayer, centering, visualizations, affirmations, looking "deeply" and "mindfully", and much more.[6] You might also want to learn more about the world of dreams. The sleeping mind is removed from the realm of the rational mind and can often be a source of great intuitive information. How often have we said to ourselves, "The idea came to me in a dream"?

Recently at a dinner party I was talking to a medical doctor whose hobby was sculpting. He told me that he had been very troubled about how to attach the extended arm of a twelve-foot statue of a figure that he was creating. He had racked his brain and simply couldn't come up with an answer. It was only in a dream that the answer finally came to him. Imagine that! He was able to achieve his objective easily and effortlessly as a result of the information he obtained in his dream, but couldn't obtain through his rational, logical, and analytical mind. I might add that the excitement on his face as he told this story was quite revealing. It was as though he had discovered a new world.

It is here that the expression "Sleep on it" makes perfect sense. As the confused mind is relaxed, the answers can seep in from somewhere in the Universe. Too often, the analytical mind can't handle the complexity of the situation, but when the analytical mind is at rest, the intuitive mind can work its miracles.

A timely story: As I began writing this chapter, I made a mental note to find a book about dreams to recommend to you. I had none to suggest, since the world of dreams is not an area that I have explored in great detail. I kid you not . . . what was the first gift I opened at my birthday dinner one week later? A book entitled, *The Dream Sourcebook and Journal: A Guide to the Theory and Interpretation of Dreams!*[7] Incredible, isn't it?

Somehow the radio wave, "Susan needs a book on dreams," was in the "air." And my dear friends, Bill Bast and Paul Huson, picked up the message. They picked it up intuitively, of course, because I had mentioned to absolutely nobody in this world that I needed a book on dreams! And to make it all the more interesting, Paul is the author of the fascinating and informative book, *How to Test and Develop Your ESP.*[8]

3) *Stop Being a Know-It-All:* As I pointed out in Chapter 2, a know-it-all retains a rigid stance. Rigidity doesn't allow the flow of intuition to course through your body or your

mind. Remember that there is so much the rational mind doesn't really know in terms of the Grand Design that it staggers the imagination. How could we possibly know it all? By definition, know-it-alls close the door to knowing. What could be more limiting than that?

4) *Create "Intention":* A strong intention is an amazing thing. It is one way of sending out those radio waves for what it is you want. When Mark and I were looking for a house in Los Angeles, there was an apartment building that had a particular view that we yearned to have. The problem was that we didn't want an apartment; we wanted a house. Nevertheless, each time I looked at the apartment building, I kept saying, "I want that view. I want that view. I want that view." Yes, I'm very persistent!

One day, I was driving in front of the "view" apartments and saw some houses on the other side of the road. I had not seen them before, as they were partially hidden from the road. What caught my eye this time was a FOR SALE sign in front of one of them. The house, of course, had the exact view that I wanted. Within a very short time, the house—and the view— was ours.

I believe that when you have a strong intention, you set energy in motion. Energy in motion touches other energy in motion and remarkable things can happen. It is important to note, however, that implied in my wish for the particular view was the understanding,

"If it is for my highest good, I will have it. If it is not for my highest good, I won't."

This understanding would have kept me from being disappointed if things hadn't turned out the way I wanted them to. The concept of highest good is a very important one to keep in mind.

I've been asked if intuition always works for our highest good. As I said earlier, no one really understands how intuition operates. But my experience has shown me that when I trust that I will be led to what is for my highest good, I'm never disappointed.

5) *Ask "Wide" Questions:* What is a "wide" question? It is a question that tunes us in to the Universe, as well as our inner intelligence. I learned three of my favorite "wide" questions from *A Course in Miracles.*[9] They are:

"Where would you have me go?"
"What would you have me do?"
"What would you have me say, and to whom?"[9]

While *A Course in Miracles* tells you to ask these questions in the morning and then go about your day, I suggest you do it *throughout* the day—at least in the beginning. You may want to surround yourself with notes reminding you to do so. Again, how quickly we forget!

6) *Turn the Questions over to Your Subconscious Mind:* Don't try to answer these questions on a rational level; let your subconscious mind take over. "Subconscious mind . . . take over, please!" Yes, I say that to myself very often.

For example, you are confused as to what to do about a certain situation. Just turn it over to your subconscious mind and put it out of your rational, conscious mind. The answer will come often when it is least expected. The rational mind is very limited and hasn't a clue as to where you should go, to whom you should speak, and what you should say. The subconscious mind has a much better connection to the Grand Design. So just turn it over and go about your day or night.

7) *Get Out of Your Own Way:* It was from the teachings of the Spiritual teacher Ram Dass that I found a perfect exercise for getting out of my own way. When I know I will be faced with having to make any decision, large or small, instead of lamenting, "What should I do?", I ask myself a much more peaceful question, "I wonder what Susan is going to do?", and, in my mind, I move on to other things. Ultimately, I find myself effortlessly acting on the decision.

Why does this work so well? The question "What should I do?" involves all kinds of logical reasoning. It involves lamenting, going back and forth between the pros and cons, taxing the rational mind. When I say, "I wonder what Susan is going to do?", I become the observer rather than the decision maker and I let my subconscious mind take over. *I distance myself from the drama.* I relax and trust that I will be led by the wisdom within me and I put the issue out of my mind. Later, I watch myself "living into" the answer.

8) *Listen to the Whispers:* Once you ask your questions, catch the thoughts that whisper in your brain. "Go to the New

School" was a whisper in my brain. And I am grateful that I was listening. The reason it is so important to quiet the mind is that you can't hear these "whispers" with a mind filled with chatter. But the quiet mind can be a wonderful receiver. And if we focus on learning how to listen to the "gap between our thoughts," the intuitive answers will come.

It helps to have a miniature tape recorder or pen and pad available at all times. For example, how often do we wake up in the middle of the night with the perfect answer to a question we have asked ourselves and then have it disappear from consciousness in the morning? Or how often when talking to a friend at dinner does the solution to a problem pop into our heads while we are discussing a totally different subject . . . and again, we forget it by the time we arrive home? My writer friends and I have little pads of paper all over the place because of the unexpected thoughts that come from who-knows-where.

Also, it is important to listen to cues you are given—a book mentioned by a friend, something said on a television broadcast, or a billboard that seems to have a very important message for you. Years ago, an airline commercial that simply said, "Get into this world!" changed my life. I felt it was an important message for me and, thankfully, I heeded it.

9) *Take Action on Your Intuitive Thoughts:* Listen to the whispers that come into your mind, often in the form of instructions to take action, then take action. Sometimes you may just get the "urge" to call a friend or a business contact, or buy a book that falls off the shelf, or whatever. That urge is

your intuition speaking. Again, see where these urges take you.

I have found that when I listen to my intuition and take action, I am led to places I never would have gone to had I listened only to the logic of my rational mind. The New School is just one example of many. What begins to happen is that you go through the day realizing that you aren't making decisions on a conscious level, rather, you are acting out of a force within and around you. Remember that intuition can be valuable as an instruction simply to call a friend or an instruction to totally change your life! Pay attention to it all.

**N O T E :** **It is important that when you take action, you act responsibly; that is, you do not take any actions that could be harmful to yourself or others.** *Even though intuitive messages are often irrational to the logical mind, they are never irresponsible.*

10) *Learn the Value of Procrastination:* When you don't really know what to do, it may be wise to do nothing! That is, procrastinate. I know "procrastination" has a negative connotation, but used in this context, it is a positive action. So many times we act as a result of fear, impatience, or other negative emotions. We want to get it resolved right now . . . fast. In such cases, it is wise to be still. Don't look for an answer in your mind, wait for an answer in your gut. So practice not making any decisions when you are confused. Let your intuition make the decision for you. Again, very often the solution pops into your head when it is least expected.

11) *Don't Try Too Hard to Find the Answers:* If we try too hard to do anything, we get in our own way. Therefore, don't try too hard to get an intuitive answer. By definition, intuition is more about flow. "Trying too hard" and "flow" simply don't go together. Instead, turn your trust over to your subconscious mind with the "knowing" that the answer will come . . . maybe in the middle of the night, maybe driving your car, maybe tonight, maybe in three years . . . but it will come.

12) *Don't Analyze:* You can see why it is important not to analyze the messages we get. If I had analyzed the "Go to the New School" message in my head, for example, I never would have investigated. Act purely on an inner trust. If you are a bit skeptical that intuition actually exists, then act simply out of curiosity . . . out of wonder. "I wonder where this thought is leading me." Somehow, something or someone somewhere is speaking to you. Aren't you curious?

While our rational mind may not have accurate information, there seems to be a part of us that does. That's the part in touch with higher and wider aspects of the world, much higher and wider than the analytical mind can go. Therefore, we can't trust only the logical mind, the rational mind, to make our decisions; we also need to develop a trust in the intuitive mind.

13) *Expand Your Energy:* You need to think wider and higher when it comes to the flow of your life. It is interesting that the symbol of intuition is sometimes the eagle, a bird that can see long and far at very great heights. We must

expand into the Universe, like the eagle, and preferably, beyond. Keep remembering that our energy doesn't end where our skin ends. Our task is to keep expanding our energy so that we can tune in to all that we need to know.

One way I love to do this is to close my eyes and imagine myself breathing in the Light from the Universe until I am totally filled with Light. I perceive this as my connection with a Higher Energy. I use this energy to lead me. I also practice transmitting this loving Light to the world around me so that I can, in some way, be a healing force in the world. The Light is always there, so I can keep giving and giving and giving it away. It's a beautiful way of being connected to the world.

14) *Be Flexible and Fluid:* Getting rid of your rigidity helps you see wider and higher. If you are obsessed that things have to be a certain way, you don't see the doors opening up all around you. Remember if it isn't one way, there's always another that may be even more fulfilling to who you are as a human being. If you are not flexible and fluid, you can't take advantage of other opportunities. You can't even see other possibilities. When you are out of the tunnel of your rigid plans and expectations, you can then see higher and see wider. By definition, the higher your thinking, the more you can see; the lower your thinking, the more your vision is clouded.

Again, here's an example from my own life. My plan after I received my doctorate in psychology was to become a full-time therapist. One day, a friend called and asked if I would assist him for a little while as he needed help in his job as executive director of (you guessed it) the Floating Hospital. At first, I said no. In fact, I had already found some work at a mental health facility. He persisted, however, and I agreed to come and help him, just for a little while. As you now recognize from an earlier chapter . . .

I relaxed my consciousness . . . I un-set my heart . . . I wore the world as a loose garment . . . I went with the flow.

Within a few months, my friend resigned and I was handed his job as executive director! Whoops! I certainly didn't expect that. I had expected to help him for a few months and then return to my original plan. And besides, I didn't feel I was qualified to be the director of anything! Thankfully, however I stayed and embraced the new challenge.

Trust me when I tell you, it was a challenge like none other that I have ever had. I went through some very difficult times, as well as many wonderful times. It was the difficult times that pulled up my power and it was the wonderful times that taught me about gratitude and joy.

And I learned from it all . . . especially the difficult times. When I left the job after ten years to become an author and an educator, I was so empowered by the experience that I remember commenting to a friend that I could be the president of the United States and handle it all. If I had been interested in politics, I might have gone for it! It goes without saying (but I'm saying it anyway), that the ten years I was involved with the Floating Hospital were filled with riches beyond my wildest dreams.

Becoming the executive director of the Floating Hospital wasn't in my life plan, but I am thankful that I was flexible enough to have been open to the experience. This doesn't mean that if I had taken the other route, I wouldn't have found great learning and joy as well; it's just that extraordinary experiences can be missed if we do not remain open and flexible as new and unexpected opportunities appear right before our eyes.

15) *Practice. Practice. Practice:* I've been asked "How does one know if it is intuition speaking or if it is the logical mind disguising itself as intuition?" In the beginning, it may be hard to know. For example, recently many people (including me) had "intuited" that they were going to win millions of dollars in the lottery. But only one person won. What happened? Obviously, this so-called intuitive feeling in the rest of us was based on a deep, deep wish, NOT intuitive guidance! The following quotation hits the nail on the head . . .

We need to act intuitively, that is, to act spontaneously from a heart that is tamed of desire and craving.[10]

Unfortunately, many of us (again, including me), are at times filled with desire and craving, thus explaining the erroneous "intuitive" feeling that we were going to win the lottery!

Also there are times when your intuition seems to be

leading you toward something that feels uncomfortable. In such a case, consider the possibility that this may be another example of intuition being mistaken for some other emotional factor . . . such as anger. Discomfort in the gut often signifies that your hunch is definitely the direction NOT to go . . . that you would, in fact, be going against the grain of what is for your highest good. This is why experimentation is necessary, especially in the beginning. Again, let me repeat that your goal is to act responsibly . . . that you take no actions that could be harmful to yourself or others.

So you need to practice, practice, practice. Experiment with little things. If you get an internal message to call someone and it makes no sense, call him or her anyway. If your mind sends the message, go right, then go right. See where you are being "led." Or read a book that seems to jump out at you in the bookstore. And, if you want to buy that lottery ticket, go buy it anyway! You get the idea. Whether you realize it or not, you use intuition every day of your life. Up until this point, you may not have noticed. Begin noticing now.

Understand that developing an intuitive sense is an exciting practice that you continue to develop for the rest of your life. It requires some patience in the beginning. Don't forget, you have to get beyond your habitual way of thinking in order to enter the world of intuition. And habits are hard to change.

Also remember that few of us become proficient at using our intuition all of the time, but we can learn to become proficient at using it a lot of the time. When you can make your intuition more of a guide in your life, you will be taken to new and exciting places. The choices of the rational mind are much more predictable; the intuitive mind is much more exciting as it can take you to places that your limited mind could never have imagined.

From the above, you can see that in an ideal world, we would never have to make any decisions. Our intuitive mind, which is filled with wisdom, would make them for us. In an ideal world, we would know exactly what to do, what to say, and to whom. In an ideal world, we would "live into" our lives in a very easy, flowing manner. Of course, most of us do not live in an ideal world, but we can have a great deal of fun working to make it one. So practice, practice, practice and have fun with that wonderful intuitive mind of yours.

I've just scratched the surface when it comes to intuition. You can continue learning more by exploring the related worlds of coincidences, synchronicity, dreams, extrasensory perception (ESP), clairvoyance, and telepathy. I encourage you to do this, as the world of intuition is a fascinating one, to be sure.

As I end this chapter, I realize that you may still be one of those who believe that "If you can't see it, it doesn't exist." I can understand your hesitance, but think about this. My husband and I were recently driving from Los Angeles to Las Vegas. Mark remembered that he needed to talk to his sister in England about an important matter. He took his teeny tiny cell phone out of his pocket, pressed a button or two, and within seconds was talking to his sister in England. Think of the "miracle" of it all: There we were in the desert, driving in our car, and Mark was talking to his sister in England! This little wireless device sent a signal and connected to another signal. Can you see the connection? (Pardon the pun.) Why do we have a hard time believing that we, too, are capable of sending out signals from within our being? Or that we are not receiving signals?

Certainly we, as human beings, are far more complex, sophisticated, and worldly than a cell phone! I could understand this doubt in a time when there was no electricity, no phones, no television, no computers, no e-mail, no chips, etc. But with such miracles of technology, why wouldn't we believe that the most advanced piece of equipment in the world . . . the human body . . . is not capable of picking up signals from all over the world . . . and beyond. We just have to psychically plug ourselves into the infinite amount of energy that exists within and around us. It is so staggeringly large that it takes my breath away!

I suggest that even if you are skeptical, it would serve you well to play with intuition, experiment with it, and have fun with it. I believe that ultimately you will join those brilliant scientists who truly believe we are all part of the Universal energy, and that we can tune in to this incredible energy at will. As you explore, you will discover that, yes, the rational mind is important, but in the end, the "gut" has to have the final say. To be sure, it has a much greater, more intelligent, and certainly more enlightened view of the world . . . and beyond.

look further look further look further look further
look further look further look further look further
look further look further look further look further
look further look further look further look further
look further look further look further look further
look further look further look further **look further**
look further look further look further look further
look further look further look further look further
look further look further look further look further
look further look further look further look further
look further look further look further look further
**look further** look further look further look further
look further look further look further look further
look further look further look further look further
look further look further look further look further
look further look further look further look further
look further look further **look further** look further
look further look further look further look further
look further look further look further look further
look further look further look further look further
look further look further look further look further
look further look further look further look further
look further look further look further look further
look further look further look further look further
look further look further look further look further
look further look further look further look further
look further look further look further look further
look further look further look further look further
look further look further look further look further
look further **look further** look further look further

look further look further look further look further
look further look further look further look further
look further look further look further look further
look further look further look further look further
look further look further look further look further
look further look further look further look further
look further look further look further look further
look further look further look further look further
look further look further look further look further
look further look further look further look further
look further look further look further look further
look further look further look further look further
look further look further look further look further
look further look further look further look further
look further look further look further look further
look further look further look further look further
look further look further look further look further
look further look further look further look further
look further look further look further look further
look further look further look further look further
look further look further look further look further
look further look further look further look further
look further look further look further look further
look further look further look further look further
look further look further look further look further
look further look further look further look further
look further look further look further look further
look further look further look further look further
look further look further look further look further
look further look further look further look further
look further look further look further look further
look further look further look further look further
look further look further look further look further

# 5

## Embracing the Learning

∞

*Barn's burnt down—now I can see the moon.*

—ZEN MASTER MASAHIDE[1]

The above quotation from Masahide delivers a compelling message. He looked at what some would consider misfortune and created in his mind a thing of beauty. He could have said to himself, as many of us would today, "How terrible. I can't believe how unlucky I am. What am I going to do now? I'll sue whoever started this fire!" Does this sound familiar? But Masahide was able to embrace the good. "Wow! I never realized how much beauty I can see with no barn to obstruct my vision. How lucky I am!" It stands to reason that . . .

> If we embrace the good that can come from whatever life hands us, we have come a long way in learning how to embrace uncertainty.

Of course, few of us respond to difficulties in such an enlightened manner. Yet, some of us do. For example, Robin Silverman, in her book, *The Ten Gifts*, talks of her home being totally destroyed in a flood. She says . . .

My worst fear, that somehow everything that mattered could be taken from me, had come true. IT WAS THE MOST LIBERATING MOMENT OF MY LIFE.[2]

Like Masahide, Silverman lost her house and chose to find the beauty instead of lamenting the loss. Of course, she faced some difficult times, but through it all, she chose to find the many "gifts" that allowed her to create a life filled with peace and meaningful activity.

And then there was the concession speech of Al Gore, as he let go of a long-held dream of becoming president of the United States in the year 2000 . . .

As for the battle that ends tonight, I do believe as my father once said, that no matter how hard the loss, defeat might serve as well as victory to shape the soul and let the glory out.[3]

How elevating and wise it is to think of "defeat" as a way to "shape the soul and let the glory out." His words certainly soothed my heart at the end of a very difficult election for me and all Americans. Whether the man we voted for won or lost the election, the words of Gore's father taught us that we can embrace the learning that comes from all situations in life . . . good or bad.

There is no question that life sometimes seems really rotten on an objective level. But perhaps the objective level is unimportant; it is the subjective level that determines our experience of any given situation. It is the subjective level that determines how we interpret what happens in our lives. Do we interpret something as good or do we interpret something as bad? I have noticed that when people look at all their experiences in life as a way of learning and discovering more about the world and themselves, then all their experiences— good or bad—are good! As Spiritual teacher Wingate Paine tells us . . .

Bad is how we see those experiences whose part in our growth we do not yet understand.[4]

Yes, if all our experiences are seen as a way of learning and growing, it could be said that no experience is bad. It follows that *if we can learn to see that ALL experiences in our lives can be really valuable, our worry about the future is greatly diminished.* We have come one step closer to being able to embrace all the uncertainty in our lives.

Again, I know that these are just words that can't describe the pain we feel when we find ourselves in the midst of horrendous circumstances that can envelop our lives, whether these circumstances have to do with our loved ones, our finances, our health, or the state of our world. But trust me when I tell you that . . .

You can use the principles of exploration, adventure, and discovery even in the middle of your deepest pain. *In fact, these principles are most valuable in the middle of our deepest pain.*

I say this with strong conviction, as I certainly used my divorce from my first husband and my cancer of many years ago as a time of great exploration, adventure, and discovery. More recently, I have used the principles of exploration, adventure, and discovery in the midst of a frightening experience with my eyes.

I was sitting at my computer when, all of a sudden, the vision through my right eye became very blurred. A rushed visit to the eye specialist revealed that a blood clot in the central vein had damaged my eye. He had no idea if it would ever heal completely. I think that all of us, whether we write books or not, dread losing our sight. And dread is the initial feeling I had when my vision went all blurred. But in the middle of my fear and upset I kept asking myself, "I wonder what this eye problem is and what I am going to learn from it." After a massive number of tests, the doctors couldn't come up with anything that would physically have caused the clot in my eye. So I began looking at my life. I didn't have to look far to come up with some reasons this eye problem might (or might not) have occurred.

Overwork? Yes. Too much intense focus on a computer screen? Yes. Stress? Yes. Paying too much attention to those things in life that aren't really important in the grand scheme of things? Yes. Physically, something had gone wrong, but what this cye scare created was a great incentive for me to look at and evaluate my life and determine what I really wanted it to look like.

What I noticed was that my life had gone off-balance, as it tends to from time to time, and it would be wise to put it back into harmony once again. I started making the necessary adjustments, and I can report that I've been enjoying life much more ever since. As I write this, the blurriness is still there, but it is not as bad as it was before. The pessimists say it will never get any better; the optimists say it will. But I live with the wondering, knowing that whether my eye does or doesn't get any better, I will handle it all.

Don't think that the eye problem was not initially upsetting to me. It was. But I also knew there were various ways in which I could approach the uncertainty of it all. I could have approached it through the thinking of my Lower Self, which produces an attitude of defeat, or through the thinking of my Higher Self, which produces an attitude of victory. It looks like this:

*An Attitude of Defeat:* I will go blind. I need my vision to live a meaningful life. What if I can't see out of that eye again? What if I lose the sight in the other eye? I can't live without my sight.

*An Attitude of Victory:* What is this problem trying to tell me? Maybe my life is out of balance and I need to be stop working so hard. Maybe more walks on the beach and time with people I love are needed in my life. I can see that I really needed a warning that my life is off course and this is a great warning!

You can see the doom and gloom and defeat in the first attitude and the possibilities for great learning in the second. This is not to say that my initial reflex reaction was to jump to the attitude of victory but, because I've been training myself over the years to embrace the good in all things, I was able to switch over to the attitude of victory in a very short time. I was able to make this switch by dipping into the box of tools that pull me up when life tries to pull me down.

For example, one of the tools that always helps me in times of difficulty is the positive affirmation. In the midst of my fear of losing my sight, I was calmed down considerably by repeating over and over again one of my favorite affirmations . . .

Whatever happens in my life, I'll handle it.

By "I'll handle it," I mean . . .

"I will learn from it. I will grow from it. I will find a way to make it enrich my life."

This means that, *even if I were to lose my sight*, "I will learn from it. I will grow from it. I will find a way to make it enrich my life."

You can see why these are magical words for embracing

uncertainty. You don't worry as much about the future when you know you can handle anything. It stands to reason that knowing what the future holds isn't as important when you know you can handle it all. When we know that we can enrich our lives with anything that happens to us . . . good or bad . . . all is well. I have certainly learned that it was in the handling of very difficult things in my life that gave me so much of the strength I find in myself today.

Also, I have a habit of telling people in the midst of their upset that "It's all happening perfectly." It is a wonderful phrase for infusing in oneself an attitude of victory. I know it truly annoys many people when they can't see anything that's "perfect" in what's happening in their lives, but I keep saying it to them anyway. Eventually they either start laughing or they want to hit me over the head! It certainly is one affirmation I repeat to myself over and over again when things are not going well. If you have read my previous books you would have seen something like the following . . .

> It's all happening perfectly.
> It's all happening perfectly.
> It's all happening perfectly.
> It's all happening perfectly.
> It's all happening perfectly.
> It's all happening perfectly.
> It's all happening perfectly.
> It's all happening perfectly.
> It's all happening perfectly.
> It's all happening perfectly.

I keep repeating it until I rightfully convince myself that I will find reason, learning, and growth in whatever is happening. In this way, I learn to "see the moon," as Masahide did, even with my blurred vision! More and more, I am learning that while I have little control in the outside world, I have much control in the "inside" world. And thoughts such as "It's all happening perfectly," give me that inner power.

What helps me believe that "It's all happening perfectly" is that I am convinced that underneath all the seeming chaos in our lives, there is a pattern, a plan . . . the Grand Design, as I love to call it. You might be surprised to learn that the scientific term, "chaos," refers to an underlying interconnectedness that exists in apparently random events. John Briggs and David Peat tell us that . . .

Chaos science focuses on hidden patterns, nuance, the "sensitivity" of things, and the "rules" for how the unpredictable leads to the new.[5]

When you can think of chaos as a pattern emerging, you can understand how it is actually happening perfectly! Thinking in this way makes it so much easier to relax, sit back, and watch the pattern and the plan emerge instead of feeling vulnerable to the seeming chanciness of all life.

Can you now see that if you can turn your worry about all the uncertainty that envelops you into a sense of excitement and possibility, your experience of life will be greatly improved? If you can step out of the "drama" and watch the miracle of life unfold, you can ultimately see that uncertainty truly is "creativity in action."

When we learn how to embrace the learning, we have the guarantee that we are never at the negative effect of circumstances; rather, we are at the positive effect of whatever happens to us. We learn that it is all a way of learning . . .

> Illness—a way of learning
> Health—a way of learning
> Poverty—a way of learning
> Wealth—a way of learning
> Depression—a way of learning
> Joy—a way of learning

By the way, while health, wealth, and joy are great ways of learning, somehow we seem to pay much more attention to the "bad" things that happen. It occurs to me that maybe when we train ourselves to pay much more attention to learning from the good things that happen, the bad won't *seem* to happen so often!

In any case, you've heard the expression, "Good stuff. Bad stuff. It's all the same stuff." The way I like to interpret this is that everything in our lives, the good and the bad, provides a great learning waiting to happen, that is, if we train ourselves to embrace the learning instead of embracing the unhappiness.

I had dinner recently with a new friend who had a stroke seven years ago while in his forties. He has trouble walking and his left arm is immobilized. He talked about the wondrous discoveries he has made about life as a result of his stroke. He has created an Internet business and jokes that most people working on their computers all day are just as immobile as he is! I was so heartened by his exquisite attitude of winning as opposed to losing. Obviously, his attitude of victory has allowed him to enjoy his life to the fullest.

In looking back at my own life, I see that certain things that happened wouldn't have been my choice. I'm sure you feel the same way about events in your life. But, as I said earlier, the objective view of life is unimportant. It is irrelevant. It is the subjective that counts. And when we approach all things with an uplifting attitude, by definition, we truly are lifted up.

I don't want to minimize the horrors of a very difficult world. Children murdered in school; a husband killed at work; people dying of cancer. Yes, it all seems terrible. But we can't help but notice that some people hold on to their grief and rage; others pull themselves up and learn from whatever happens to them in life. They embrace even the horror. *They choose an attitude of victory.* I know we would all prefer to learn all we need to know from having only joyful experiences, but, as you will discover in the next chapter, our most profound learning often comes from the difficult experiences.

I have no clue as to why the powers-that-be forgot to include one important feature in the design of the human being . . . the information we need to know in order to have a worry-free and stress-free life. It seems we all, including the Buddha, Christ, and all Spiritual leaders, have to go through many periods of great trial and tribulation in order to reach that desirable state of enlightenment . . . that understanding that "All is well" despite what is happening in the world around and within us. To reach that state of "All is well" in the midst of our thinking about the present and the future is indeed a state of grace.

So, since we aren't born with worry-free minds, we have to take the responsibility to transform ourselves in this area. And again, we do this by re-visioning our mind, that is, breaking the habit of seeing things with an attitude of defeat and retraining ourselves to see things with an attitude of victory. All of the exercises in this book are designed to help us do that. Here are a few more to help us embrace the learning . . . which ultimately helps us to embrace the inevitable uncertainty in all our lives.

---

## THE "I CAN LEARN FROM THIS" EXERCISE

You're going to hate me for this exercise. In fact, you'd better do it with a friend, so at least you can have a lot of laughs together. The goal is to respond to all that is happening in your life as perfection in action. It goes like this . . .

The food stinks . . . . . . . . . . . . . *I can learn from this.*
My date was horrible. . . . . . . . . *I can learn from this.*
My wallet was stolen . . . . . . . . . *I can learn from this.*

I told you that you'd hate me for this one! Obviously the purpose of this exercise is to teach you that you can learn from all things. Remember that your experience of life reflects how you see the world. It is better to see it from a place of learning than a place of misery!

Of course, when we realize "I can learn from this" with the little things in life, it makes it much easier to realize we can learn from the bigger things in life. When we have the phrase, "I can learn from this," firmly imprinted on our minds we can react much more positively to the experiences in life that bring us pain . . .

I lost my job . . . . . . . . . . . . . . *I can learn from this.*
I lost my relationship. . . . . . . . . *I can learn from this.*
My best friend died. . . . . . . . . . *I can learn from this.*

Once we realize that we can learn from all things, our goal then is to focus on the learning, that is, to focus on the good instead of the bad.

Let's take this exercise one step further. I said that very often we fail to notice that the good in our lives can serve as a great learning experience as well. How about this?

I got the job . . . . . . . . . . . . . . . *I can learn from this.*
I am loved . . . . . . . . . . . . . . . . *I can learn from this.*
I love my friends . . . . . . . . . . . *I can learn from this.*

When we focus on the learning from all that is wonderful in our lives, we enlarge the magnitude of the blessings and can create an enhanced sense of joy. Always remember we can learn from it all . . . the good and the bad.

Your next step is to add this important sentence, "I can learn from this," to the events you reported in Part 3 of the I Wonder exercise in Chapter 1. For example . . .

> I had a great lunch with Lydia. I really enjoy being with her. I can learn from this.
>
> My meeting with my boss didn't go well at all. I think I'd better "feel the fear and do it anyway," and get a new job! It's time! I can learn from this.
>
> I saw the movie *Schindler's List,* and it was great. I cried through the whole picture. I can learn from this.
>
> Dinner with Bob was a bit tense. I wonder if he'll call again. I can learn from this.

Once you create an intent to learn, it is reassuring how much you actually can learn! Instead of focusing on the doom and gloom, your body, mind, and heart are focused on the learning. Sometimes the learning happens immediately; sometimes it takes a little while. But when you are focused and have a strong intent, the learning will inevitably come.

## THE "THIS TOO SHALL PASS" EXERCISE

It is important to focus on the reality of cycles. Good follows bad and bad follows good. Life is a series of ups and downs. It is important not to identify with the ups and downs of life;

rather, we must learn how to step outside ourselves and just notice. We must not be attached to the good; we must not be depressed by the bad. The ups and downs are just part of the flow of life.

There is no use trying to change the order of the Universe . . . it won't work. Sorry about that! You can't get rid of the downs and you can't hold on to the ups. It's much better to notice both with the understanding that "This too shall pass." When things are wonderful . . . this too shall pass. When things are difficult . . . this too shall pass. Once you have this recognition, you are much more relaxed about events in your life.

It helps to get this harmonious flow of life imprinted in your brain by watching what is happening in your life and consciously "noticing" that it is all temporary, that is, this too shall pass. For example . . .

I feel great today . . . . . . . . . . . . . . *this too shall pass.*
I feel horrible today . . . . . . . . . . . . *this too shall pass.*
The weather is great . . . . . . . . . . . . *this too shall pass.*
The weather is horrible . . . . . . . . . . *this too shall pass.*

It is more difficult, but perhaps more important, to do this exercise with more meaningful parts of our lives, for example, with our relationships. As I mentioned earlier, I absolutely adore my husband and our wonderful life together. But I know that death comes to all of us and the day will come when we won't be together any longer. I joke that since today's statistics suggest that women live seven years longer than men, I married a man seven years younger so that we can die on the same day! But who knows what the future holds?

The way my husband and I handle the reality that "This too shall pass" is to truly enjoy the time we have together. We appreciate each other and fill ourselves up with the love we feel for each other. We both know that "This too shall pass " but this knowing keeps us from putting off enjoying our life together, rather than taking it for granted. As I will discuss later in this book, the art of appreciation is important in helping us embrace the uncertainty in all areas of our lives.

So, beginning today, imprint the words, "This too shall pass," in your mind. It is an important thought. And, as I suggest you do with all important thoughts and affirmations, write it on a little card and place it wherever you can see it as a constant reminder. Yes, my desk is filled with such reminders!

As you use the valuable exercises I provide throughout this chapter and throughout the book, know that embracing uncertainty doesn't happen all at once. It is a process. It takes a retraining of the mind to get us to the place of peace. Also, a lot of the retraining is trial and error. Understand that when something is not going the way you want it to go, it doesn't mean that it is going wrong or that you did something wrong. It means it's going right. All you have to do is set your sights on learning everything you can learn. And one day it will all fit into place.

It goes without saying that if we approach life with a sense of dire consequences, we close out so much of the possibility that is inherently there. But when we approach all of life with an intent to learn and grow, we can see wider and farther than we ever thought possible.

A final note: As I write these words, many of us in the USA and throughout the world, consciously or unconsciously, are discovering how to embrace the learning in the aftermath of the horrific terrorist attack on the World Trade Center and the Pentagon. Initially, our eyes saw only the horror of the pain and loss of life experienced by so many innocent people. But, in a remarkably short time, this sense of horror was superseded by an awesome feeling of love, unity, caring, giving, helping, and a profound determination that we shall learn and grow from it all.

In my entire life, I have never experienced such an unimaginable sense of love and togetherness. I witnessed so many ordinary people acting in such extraordinary ways. I thought to myself, "Wow! This is what a nation truly united in love actually looks like! How spectacular!" I know I was not alone in my thoughts.

I also know these intense feelings of unity will diminish as time passes and as we move on with our lives, but at some level our lives have been permanently transformed by the sense of unity we experienced and the vision of so many heroes giving so much. One only has to look to the policemen, the firemen, and so many others who would have given their lives . . . and many did . . . to save the lives of others. The words "Thank you" are on all of our lips as we take in the true meaning of giving.

An unimaginable horror? Yes. An unimaginable outpouring of love and caring? Yes. Who knows if more acts of terrorism will follow? Maybe they will; maybe they won't. But as we focus on the love, learning, and growing that can come from it all, we actually become less afraid, knowing that we will come out of it stronger and more alive with the possibility of becoming a more meaningful part of the world . . . each of us in our own way.

**be a hero** be a hero be a hero be a hero be a hero be a hero be a hero be a hero be a hero be a hero be a hero be a hero be a hero be a hero be a hero be a hero be a hero be a hero be a hero be a hero be a hero be a hero be a hero be a hero be a hero be a hero be a hero be a hero be a hero be a hero be a hero be a hero be a hero be a hero be a hero be a hero be a hero be a hero **be a hero** be a hero be a hero be a hero be a hero be a hero be a hero be a hero be a hero be a hero be a hero be a hero be a hero be a hero be a hero be a hero be a hero be a hero be a hero be a hero be a hero be a hero be a hero be a hero be a hero be a hero be a hero be a hero be a hero be a hero be a hero be a hero be a hero be a hero be a hero be a hero be a hero be a hero be a hero be a hero be a hero be a hero be a hero be a hero **be a hero** be a hero be a hero be a hero be a hero be a hero be a hero be a hero be a hero be a hero be a hero be a hero be a hero be a hero be a hero be a hero be a hero be a hero be a hero be a hero be a hero be a hero be a hero be a hero be a hero be a hero be a hero be a hero be a hero be a hero be a hero be a hero be a hero be a hero be a hero be a hero be a hero be a hero be a hero **be a hero** be a hero be a hero be a hero be a hero be a hero be a hero be a hero be a hero be a hero be a hero be a hero be a hero be a hero be a hero be a hero be a hero be a hero be a hero be a hero be a hero be a hero be a hero be a hero be a hero be a hero be a hero be a hero be a hero be a hero be a hero be a hero be a hero be a hero be a hero be a hero be a hero be a hero be a hero be a hero be a hero be a hero be a hero be a hero be a hero be a hero be a hero be a hero be a hero **be a hero** be a hero

# 6

## Collecting Heroes

∞

*Freedom is like a gem which shines with equal
brilliance in all surroundings; it gleams
as well in mud as on velvet.*

—ALAN W. WATTS[1]

To me, a sense of freedom comes from the ability to live in the Higher Self no matter what is happening in your life. That's right, *no matter what is happening in your life.* In the last chapter, I talked about embracing the learning instead of drowning in the negativity of any given situation. Here, I'm going to turn up the volume and show you how some who have experienced *the very worst* life has to offer have made something profoundly uplifting and enriching out of it all. They had the choice of seeing themselves as a "victim" or seeing themselves as a "winner" of valuable life experiences. They chose the latter and the result is a magnificent lesson for us all. And that lesson is. . . .

If they can learn and grow *from the worst that life has to offer,* we can learn and grow from *anything* that life offers us!

These individuals become our models—our heroes—showing us the immense strength of the human body and the human spirit. They give us courage as we realize that if they were able to valiantly face the extreme difficulties life handed them, we too can face anything that comes our way. We can ask for no better insurance policy when living in such an uncertain world.

It is my privilege now to introduce you to just a few of my favorite heroes. You will be very moved and inspired by their stories. What unites them all is that they have learned how to use their suffering as Spiritual practice . . . as a way to learn, to grow, to teach, and to shine. They have learned how to transcend the victim mentality and touch the best of who they are.

(NOTE: I suggest you read their stories OVER . . . AND OVER . . . AND OVER again. Trust me when I tell you that you will become stronger and more inspired with each reading.)*

∞

If you are familiar with my previous work, you will know that **Viktor Frankl** is one of my heroes. I have talked about Viktor Frankl briefly in other contexts, but nowhere are his stagger-

---

*I certainly became stronger and more inspired as I created this chapter. And each read-through in the editing process left a deeper and deeper impression within my being.

ingly powerful ideas more relevant than they are here. He is an incredible example of how a person can embrace uncertainty in the worst that life can bring us.

In case you haven't heard of Viktor Frankl, he was a man whose father, mother, wife, and brother all perished in the concentration camps of World War II. Somehow he survived. The concentration camp was a world that consisted of starvation, freezing cold, disease, gas chambers, crematoriums, and massacres. Seemingly unbearable. The concentration camp was also a world that took away one's entire former life. There was NOTHING left. I know this all sounds depressing, but stay with me. I know you will be uplifted when you see how beauty was to be found even in the middle of such horror.

Let me give you a taste of the learning that Viktor Frankl embraced and, thankfully, passed on to us all:[2]

- Frankl discovered that a person can get used to anything . . . mentally and physically. No matter how horrible, no matter how punishing, and no matter how grotesque the situation, the human Spirit can survive . . . better yet, the human Spirit can reign triumphant.

- The horror of the situation was not Soul-destroying for everyone; to some it was "Soul-awakening," which allowed them to retreat from the horrors around them "to a life of inner riches and spiritual freedom."[3] Note that Frankl is not talking about religion here; he is talking about belief in one's meaning and purpose. (I'll discuss that further in the next chapter.) For him, this offered an explanation as to why some who were less robust survived *better* than those who were stronger.

- Humor was actually in evidence in such a horrible place. Frankl talked about humor as one of the Soul's weapons in the fight for self-preservation. Why? Because it allowed those who were imprisoned to take a step away from the drama, even if only for a few minutes.

- Curiosity was evident as well . . . curiosity as to what would be the outcome of it all. As with humor, curiosity helped to separate people's minds from the drama and allowed them to become more observers than victims. Ah, yes . . . the wonder of wondering.

- Appreciation increased. Just watching a beautiful bird on the prison fence was a deeply moving experience. A piece of bread could create a feeling of intense joy and comfort. The smallest of blessings produced the greatest of pleasures . . . much more so than when the prisoners lived a "normal" life.

- Generosity was shiningly in evidence, such as when some people gave away their last piece of bread to those who needed it more. This didn't describe everyone, of course, but it did describe those who were able to touch the Spiritual part of who they were . . . those who lived in the Higher Self.

- And then there was the big surprise that the human body was able to withstand so many things. Even though he was trained as a doctor, Frankl concluded that the medical profession didn't know everything. You could be freezing and not get ill. You could be around disease and not get ill. You could go without much sleep and not get ill. You could receive very little nourishment and not get ill. You could be unable to clean your teeth and have a terrible vitamin deficiency and still have healthy gums. You could be unable to clean the sores on your body and remain infection-free. Remarkable!

- He learned that one could find the blessing in any situation. For example, there were those times when he did succumb to illness. At such times he would find himself lying on a hard board packed side by side with other men who were also ill. While most observers would see it as a scene from hell, Frankl said he was actually grateful that: 1) he was not out in the cold working; and 2) he was able to warm himself by the bodily heat of the men around him.

- He learned not to judge people, understanding that none of us know how we would react under similar circumstances. He noted that there were good prisoners and horrible prisoners. There were also good guards and horrible guards.

- Frankl learned a lot about love. He didn't know if his wife was still alive (she wasn't), but he discovered that "love goes very far beyond the physical person of the beloved."[4] He said that nothing could touch the strength of his love, whether his wife was alive or not.*

- Most importantly, he learned that if there is a meaning to life at all, which he believed there was, then *there was meaning in all the suffering*. Suffering is part of all of our lives. We need to learn and grow and find our purpose in it all.

Wow! This tiny taste of what Frankl learned is enough to demonstrate that one can experience intense horror and emerge with an incredible amount of power, learning, and love. This isn't to say that, initially and throughout the concentration camp experience, there weren't times everyone experienced periods of depression, hopelessness, shock, apathy, longing, and disgust, but, at some point, those who were more Spiritually evolved allowed their inner power and love to take charge of the situation and save them over and over and over again.

When we understand that we all have this awesome inner power and love, our trust in ourselves grows and grows and

---

*You will be happy to know that while Frankl lost the wife he loved so much, he remarried a number of years after his ultimate release from the camp at the end of the war. He was very happily married to his second wife for over fifty years until his death at the age of ninety-two in 1997.

our fear fades into the background. And to give you the quotation that could make all the difference in your life as it made in mine. . . .

> Everything can be taken from a man but one thing: the last of the human freedoms—to choose one's attitude in any given set of circumstances, to choose one's own way.[5]

Wow, again! We must remind ourselves every minute of the day—even if we are ill, even if we are poor, even if we are in the middle of a dilemma, or whatever life may hand us—that we have the choice to live in a state of Spiritual well-being instead of a state of misery. There is no question that suffering is a part of everyone's life . . . it's part of the human condition. And the wisest choice that we can make is to use that suffering as an opportunity to discover the very best of who we are and find the gifts in it all. In so doing, we totally release ourselves from the role of victim and become an eager student of life.

---

Thank you, Viktor Frankl, for finding the best of who you are in such horrendous circumstances and providing such an elegant and uplifting model for the rest of us to follow.

---

∞

**Ram Dass** is also a hero of mine. While he has been a great teacher to me for many, many years, he has now become my hero. For those of you who don't know who Ram Dass (aka Richard Alpert) is, in a nutshell, he is an ex-psychologist who became a famous hippie, wrote the best-selling book, *Be Here Now*, and then moved on to become a world-renowned Spiritual teacher with an amazing sense of humor.

In 1997, Ram Dass was handed an enormous challenge to the human Spirit when he suffered a debilitating stroke. For some time, he was in a state of complete physical helplessness. From being someone who identified with the role of caregiver, in an instant, he became someone who had to be totally taken care of. Having lost most of his bodily functions, there was nothing, except breathing, that he could do on his own.

It is now a number of years later, and a lot of his mobility has been restored, but he is still somewhat physically impaired. Thankfully, however, he is not Spiritually impaired . . . in fact, as you will see, he is Spiritually enriched! In his wonderful new book with the whimsical title, *Still Here*,[6] Ram Dass offers us another example of how so-called tragedy can enter one's life and, in the midst of it all, one can find the many gifts that are there for the taking.

You may be wondering what gifts Ram Dass could possibly find in a debilitating stroke. Here are a few examples. . . .

- Coming through the stroke has left him less afraid. He says, "The stroke took me through one of my deep fears and I'm here to report that 'the only thing we have to fear is fear itself.'"[7]

- Ram Dass sees himself as having two incarnations instead of one: "This is me and that was him." This keeps him from lamenting the things he can't do anymore because of the paralysis. This so beautifully demonstrates to me the principle that, just as we can't be attached to the future, we can't be attached to the past!

- Prior to the stroke, Ram Dass spent much of his time in motels as he traveled the world giving workshops and talks. After the stroke, he had to stop traveling as much and he discovered a heavenly place called HOME. And he realized what he had been missing. He is now much more content and able to sit in quiet appreciation of the beauty of life . . . the trees, the flowers, the silence, instead of being busy, busy, busy all the time.[8]

- He says that even though he can now move around with a walker, he has grown to love his wheelchair. He jokes, "Who wouldn't rather ride than walk?"[9] And his wonderful silliness comes out when he reports that he loves racing through the airport in his wheelchair yelling, "Beep-beep"!

- Words had been his life, but the stroke gave him aphasia, which makes it difficult for him to find the words he is looking for. Even with the aphasia, he has begun conducting retreats and workshops regularly again. He says that the words come slowly, but now his students can ponder his meaning in the silences between the words. Illuminating![10]

- In a talk in 1999, Ram Dass told his audience that when he had his stroke, his ego was shattered and for a while he lost his faith. But then his Soul took over. He said, "My ego said: 'Help! Chaos! Pain!'" But when his Soul took over, it viewed the whole thing as a new adventure. "How interesting!" He jokes that his Soul found the stroke very good entertainment![11]

- The damage was done to his left brain which is the more analytical part of the brain. He claims that now the right brain is freer to come out and play! As you may have already surmised from Ram Dass's claim, those with left brain dominance are more structured, intellectual, logical, serious, and the like. Those with right brain dominance are more intuitive, creative, spontaneous, and, yes, playful.

- He was a puzzlement to doctors because he was so happy most of the time. The medical profession, being somewhat Spiritually deprived, wondered how you can be happy when you've had a stroke! He told the doctors he was happy because his awareness was on a Spiritual plane, not on a worldly plane. And to the

Soul, "things like disability and pain and dependence
are just . . . poignant."[12]

- He's learned to "play" new roles. As I already mentioned, he used to get his sense of power from helping.
In fact, he wrote a book entitled, *How Can I Help?*
Now, he said, if he were to write a book, it would have
to be called, *How Can You Help Me?* I love it when he
says that "from the Soul's perspective, both helpee and
helper are just hanging out together—complementary
roles in a dance. Without us helpees, what would the
helpers have to do?"[13]

- With his usual good sense of humor and always looking for the gifts in any situation, Ram Dass was grateful that the stroke gave him an ending to the book he
was writing . . . which was about aging! Yes, *Still Here*
is a wonderful book about aging. Prior to his stroke,
Ram Dass was a vibrant mid-sixty-year-old who was
physically active and very mobile. Then he was con-
fined to a wheelchair. He couldn't have found a better
understanding of aging anywhere!

- Ram Dass feels that the difficulties in life bring
us all closer to God and a higher consciousness. One
of the many lines that brought me to tears was
this . . .

> I haven't been cured of my stroke, but I
> have definitely been *healed* by it.[14]

---

**Thank you, Ram Dass. Your wisdom and humor help us
all. You are truly magnificent.**[15]

---

∽∞

Just reading the newspaper can introduce us to many
heroes. For example, I read a story in the *Los Angeles Times*
about a hero named **Art Burg**.[16] Art Burg became a quadri-
plegic after an auto accident in 1983. Prior to the accident,
he had been a very athletic person, he was the co-owner of a
tennis court construction business, and he was engaged to
be married.

The doctors and hospital personnel told him that he
would probably never be able to do much for the rest of his
life. So much for the wisdom of the doctors and the hospital
personnel! Undaunted, Art Burg vowed that nothing would
stop him from having a wonderfully active and productive life.

Of course, at times he fought depression and pain, but in
the end, nothing did stop him. His motto became . . .

While the difficult takes time, the impossible just
takes a little longer.

In essence, he had to re-create his life, that is . . .

to dream new dreams,
to ask new questions,
and to think new thoughts.

Most importantly, he decided not to see himself as a victim and ask such silly questions as, "Why me?"

Like Viktor Frankl, Art Burg realized that he had the power to control his *reaction* to his injuries. It was all up to him as to whether he was going to see his life as a *tragedy* or as an *opportunity*. Thankfully, he chose the latter. And like Ram Dass, he was happy. Again, the medical staff was puzzled by his happiness. It was written on his medical chart that he was exhibiting "excessive happiness." Something must be wrong! They attributed his happiness to a state of denial in that he hadn't accepted the gravity of his condition. Wrong! He more than accepted it, he was empowered by it!

No matter what the situation, he never gave up. It took him a full year to be able to put on his trousers, five years to put on his socks and shoes. I could go on and on about how difficult it was for him to relearn the most basic life functions. But no matter what it was, he kept trying until he succeeded. Eventually, he learned to get around in a wheelchair, type with two fingers and answer phones. At that point, he decided it was time to return to work.

He was rejected time and time again by potential employers. They loved him on the phone, but when they saw he was in a wheelchair, he didn't get the job. Again he refused to give up. Finally, he was hired as a telephone receptionist at an IBM message center, and he set a division record. Then he was hired as a computer sales rep, and he earned three sales awards. Then he went into business himself, managing three bookstores and was named young entrepreneur of the year. In 1991, he became a motivational speaker. He talks about overcoming adversity, remaining optimistic, and maintaining self-esteem. He says . . .

> I thank God that life is hard . . . because, in the pain, the struggle, the loneliness, and the rejection, we begin to learn. And when we learn, we grow, and when we grow, a miracle happens. We begin to change.

Did you get that? *He thanks God that life is hard!* He reports that he travels 200,000 miles annually appearing at more than 150 engagements. He earns about $13,000 a speech. He received 840 speaking requests in 2000. He is a board member of the National Speakers Association. He is happily married and has two children. He has become a wheelchair athlete competing in several difficult races. He started speakers.com, which links professional speakers with speakers' bureaus. And who knows what he'll do next?

He has a clear purpose, and that is to show the world that you can make something beautiful even with a condition as difficult as his. He gets many e-mails from those who have had similar experiences and says that to share someone else's burden is a great joy.

---

Thank you, Art Burg. You truly are a hero and a shining example to us all. May you always be noted for your "excessive happiness" and may we all join you!

---

∞

Another hero of mine is **Sally Lefkowitz,** who also overcame huge physical difficulties. (As you can tell, I am in awe of people who won't let their physical handicaps get in the way of a beautiful life. Their strength and refusal to be a victim is a lesson for us all.) I met Sally during the time I was executive director of the Floating Hospital, where, lucky for me, she became a board member. In addition to her role as wife and mother, she was actively involved in contributing her time, money, and efforts to charities that helped the poor and disabled. Then one day, she had a stroke that put her permanently in a wheelchair.

I'll never forget one particular evening shortly after Sally's stroke occurred. The Floating Hospital, as its name suggests, was aboard a ship. We were having a big fund-raiser that, prior to her stroke, Sally had been very actively involved in organizing. She had invited many people to come to the event hoping they would get involved in supporting our many activities . . . as she had done. As the staff and I were preparing to welcome everyone aboard for our evening cruise around Manhattan, I felt so sorry that she would not be there to enjoy the fruits of her labors.

Just as this thought was going through my mind, I glanced toward the end of the pier. And there to my surprise and delight was Sally being wheeled down the pier by her husband. I ran to greet her, gave her a big hug, and with tears in my eyes thanked her for coming. She spoke with great difficulty (she has thankfully fully recovered her speech since), but was able to convey to me that she wanted to welcome aboard the people she had invited to let them know how much the Floating Hospital meant to her.

There she was . . . unable to speak properly, her face partially paralyzed, unable to walk, still shaky and exhausted from her ordeal, but she didn't let us down. She didn't stay for the entire event, but she was there to welcome her guests and set the tone for all of us. By making this supreme effort, she let us know that what we were doing was important. And she let her guests know that what they could do to help us was also important.

Many years have passed and Sally is now in her nineties. She remains in a wheelchair, but she doesn't let that destroy her Spirit. She let's NOTHING destroy her Spirit, even the death of her wonderfully loving husband a few years after her stroke. Throughout her life, she has had almost every ailment that can befall a human being, including cancer and tuberculosis, a stroke, and she is now facing possible blindness, but NOTHING stops her from being a meaningful part of the world.

At the time of this writing she still appears at the board meetings of the various charities she supports. She still helps others in any way she can. She still enjoys the park. She still eats lunch regularly at her favorite restaurant, the Russian Tea Room. And she'll always be a role model and a hero to me. While I frequently tell her so, I want to thank her publicly. So . . .

---

Thank you, Sally Lefkowitz. I love you. You truly are a hero to me.

---

And then there is **Elian Gonzalez**. You may think that he is a strange choice for a hero: after all, he doesn't fit the criteria I set at the beginning of this chapter. That is, we don't know if he will learn how to use his suffering as Spiritual practice . . . as a way to learn, to grow, to teach, and to shine. And we don't know if he will actually transcend the victim mentality and touch the best of who he is. But he is still a hero to me.

I remember the day when this little Cuban boy was found adrift in the sea. He took over our television sets . . . and our hearts. He was an amazement to me, and I couldn't help but feel the strength of the human spirit every time his picture appeared on my television set.

While everyone was thinking, "Poor Elian," I chose to think how fortunate he was to learn so early in life how much he was able to survive. He experienced his parents' divorce. He survived alone in the sea holding on to an inner tube after his mother was swept out to the sea right before his eyes. After his rescue, he spent four months at the center of the drama involving his father, his relatives in Miami, the media, and the governments of Cuba and the United States. He was then whisked away in the middle of the night by a SWAT team to be finally reunited with his father, who took him back to his home in Cuba. And who knows where the story will go from here?

Many of us wanted him to remain in Miami with his relatives; many of us wanted him to be reunited with his father and returned to his home in Cuba. But whatever side of the drama we found ourselves on, we couldn't help but be awed by the courage of this little boy.

At the time, I heard so many psychologists say with certainty that Elian will be irreparably damaged for the rest of his life because of the difficulty he endured. (Obviously, they haven't learned the power of maybe, the value of doubt!) In truth, maybe they're right; maybe they're wrong. I am very optimistic. I fantasize about him growing up to be powerful and loving in whatever he chooses to do, knowing he has the capacity to survive so much.

Again, I don't know how that brave and beautiful child, Elian Gonzalez, will process all that happened to him and how he will use it as he grows into adulthood and beyond, but I do know that, in my mind, his status as a hero is already established.

---

Thank you, Elian Gonzalez. You truly are a jewel found in the sea.

---

∞

Now that you have met some of my heroes, you have a delicious taste of how much one can learn from the worst that life can offer. Thankfully, most of us don't have to face such extreme difficulties! In fact, the difficulties most of us face are "easy" in comparison. But even if we did have to face such extreme difficulties, we would know from our heroes that, if they can learn and grow and find the gifts in it all, so can we.

It is fitting that I end this chapter with the following two exercises designed to help you embrace the "hero mentality" instead of the "victim mentality" . . . an essential requirement for helping us embrace all the uncertainty in our own lives.

## THE "COLLECT YOUR HEROES" EXERCISE

It's now time for you to collect your own heroes . . . people you can look to when things are not going well in your own life. Stories abound of people who have made something wonderful out of the worst life can offer. You can find these stories in books, in newspaper articles, on television, in the movies, or on your own Journey through life.

To help you in your "collecting phase," ask your friends and family who they consider to be their personal heroes and why. You may get some good ideas. If you have children, make "collecting heroes" a project for all of you to enjoy. Heroes are in the air, all around you, *but you must pay attention.*

It would be helpful to create a notebook of your heroes listing what they have learned from their experience (as I have done above) so that when things are not going well, you can remind yourself over and over again . . .

If they can learn and grow from their experiences, I can certainly learn and grow from mine!

This has worked wonderfully for me. Throughout the various difficulties in my life, I had only to think of one of my

heroes, such as Viktor Frankl, who was handed circumstances that were so much more difficult than mine, and I
was able to say to myself, "If he was able to learn and grow
from his experiences, which are about the worst I can imagine, then I can learn and grow from mine."

If you can't immediately find any heroes in your life, I'll
lend you mine. But just keep looking. There are many, many
heroes in this world . . . past, present, and future. It is just a
matter of paying attention and finding the ones that "speak"
to you in terms of your own particular worries about the
future.

---

### THE "BE A HERO" EXERCISE

"Susan, how can *I* be a hero?" Trust me. You can. All of us
can. Maybe you already are and you just don't know it yet!
In any case, here are a few "How To Be a Hero" suggestions . . .

1) WHEN DIFFICULTIES ARISE, IMMEDIATELY
REJECT THE VICTIM MENTALITY AND BEGIN LOOKING
FOR THE GOOD. That is, find the blessings in any situation
you encounter . . . whether it is something little, like a traffic
jam, or something big, like a serious illness. This sends out a
wonderfully positive energy that helps not only you, but also
those around you. Conversely, when you cling to the victim
mentality, this sends out a terribly negative energy that hurts
not only you, but also hurts those around you. Not good! So
it's important to let go of the victim mentality.

As you play the game of "find the blessings", you will be amazed at the number of blessings you will find. For example, I have heard some say after going through a very difficult time in their lives . . .

"It made me stronger."
"It made me more confident."
"I'm much more Spiritual as a result of what happened."
"I used to be a spoiled brat. Now I am much more humane and compassionate."

Strength, confidence, Spirituality, compassion. You can see that when you are able to find the good, nothing seems so bad after all!

2) SHARE THE "BLESSINGS" YOU HAVE FOUND WITH OTHERS. Talk about them . . . or write about them. Others will be uplifted and encouraged by your ability to make something good from something bad. Where appropriate, get involved with or start an organization that helps the world in some way as a result of your misfortune.

As an example, Mothers Against Drunk Driving (MADD) was started by Candy Lightner and a small group of women, after the painful loss of Candy's thirteen-year-old child who had been killed by a drunk driver. MADD now has six hundred chapters across the United States and is responsible for saving many, many lives. A beautiful example of how good can come from bad.

Another example: The Polly Klaas® Foundation[17] was started by Marc Klaas, father of twelve-year-old Polly who, in 1993, was abducted from her home in Petaluma, California, and murdered. Marc Klaas was devastated, but he turned his despair into hope for himself and many others. With no prior media, political, or public speaking experience, he learned how to affect legislation and fight for children's issues. Ultimately he founded the Polly Klaas® Foundation, which has helped so many others deal with the terror that is experienced when a child is missing. The Foundation has worked on behalf of thousands of missing children and reports an average recovery rate of 85 percent. And through its educational programs, it works very hard to prevent violence against children. Marc Klaas has created so much good from a deeply tragic experience.

There are many examples of people creating wonderful things as a result of painful experiences in their lives. True heroes, to be sure . . . and there is no reason whatsoever why you can't join them in their status as a hero. It's an elevating place to be.

Just remember that, when you radiate an energy of strength and determination as you experience life's difficulties, everyone around you will be uplifted. This is not to say that you should avoid what I call the Land of Tears.[18] There are times when tears and grief are appropriate . . . even essential. But when they are the tears of the hero versus the tears of the victim, even tears and grief can give others hope. In the eyes of a hero, things may be painful for the moment, but in the end . . . all will be well.

It was how I handled my experience with breast cancer that made me a hero to some. When I discovered that I had breast cancer many years ago, I remember saying to myself, "I will find a way to make this a blessing." I couldn't imagine what blessings could possibly be found in breast cancer, but I was determined I would find them. And indeed, with a strong intention to find the blessings, I found them all over the place!

As I collected blessings, I decided to share my story of breast cancer with others . . . which turned out to be one of the greatest blessings of all. I started to write about and talk publicly about the fact that a mastectomy wasn't the end of the world; in fact, for me, it was an amazingly enriching experience. I joke that my husband calls me "his one-tit wonder!" I even got an award, aptly called the Spirit of Discovery Award, from the Associates for Breast Cancer Studies for sharing my story with so many others.[19]

The good news is that many women listened to me and they heard and they breathed a sigh of relief. To this day, it makes my heart sing to receive feedback from so many women who tell me that I have become a hero to them . . . all because of my having had breast cancer! Trust me when I tell you that . . .

Becoming a hero will not only make others stronger, it is guaranteed to make you stronger as well.

So think about all that has happened in your life and all that possibly could happen in the future and determine to make something grand from it all. In this way, you can be a hero to everyone around you . . . and most importantly . . . you can be a hero to yourself.

Yes, we all hope life gives us more good than bad. Maybe it will, maybe it won't. But when we come to the realization that we can make something good from the bad, we also come to the realization that THERE REALLY IS NO BAD! Instead, there is opportunity after opportunity to improve the quality of our inner lives by using all that life hands us to make us stronger and more loving people.

Always remember that how we live our lives is *a personal decision*, not something that is put upon us from the outside world. I trust you will decide to . . .

Live a "hero-full" life.

This is your challenge. This is your safety net. This is your guarantee. This is your peace of mind.

find your purpose find your purpose find your
purpose find your purpose find your purpose find
your purpose find your purpose find your purpose
find your purpose find your purpose find your
purpose find your purpose find your purpose find
your purpose find your purpose **find your purpose**
find your purpose find your purpose find your
purpose find your purpose find your purpose find
your purpose find your purpose find your purpose
find your purpose find your purpose find your
purpose find your purpose find your purpose find
your purpose find your purpose find your purpose
**find your purpose** find your purpose find your
purpose find your purpose find your purpose find
your purpose find your purpose find your purpose
find your purpose find your purpose find your
purpose find your purpose **find your purpose** find
your purpose find your purpose find your purpose
find your purpose find your purpose find your
purpose find your purpose find your purpose find
your purpose find your purpose find your purpose
find your purpose find your purpose find your
purpose find your purpose find your purpose find
your purpose find your purpose find your purpose
find your purpose find your purpose find your
purpose find your purpose find your purpose find
your purpose **find your purpose** find your purpose
find your purpose find your purpose find your

find your purpose find your purpose find your
purpose find your purpose find your purpose find
your purpose find your purpose find your purpose
find your purpose find your purpose find your
purpose find your purpose find your purpose find
your purpose find your purpose **find your purpose**
find your purpose find your purpose find your
purpose find your purpose find your purpose find
your purpose find your purpose find your purpose
find your purpose find your purpose find your
purpose find your purpose find your purpose find
your purpose find your purpose find your purpose
**find your purpose** find your purpose find your
purpose find your purpose find your purpose find
your purpose find your purpose find your purpose
find your purpose find your purpose find your
purpose find your purpose **find your purpose** find
your purpose find your purpose find your purpose
find your purpose find your purpose find your
purpose find your purpose find your purpose find
your purpose find your purpose find your purpose
find your purpose find your purpose find your
purpose find your purpose find your purpose find
your purpose find your purpose find your purpose
find your purpose find your purpose find your
purpose find your purpose find your purpose find
your purpose find your purpose find your purpose
find your purpose find your purpose find your
purpose find your purpose find your purpose find
your purpose **find your purpose** find your purpose
find your purpose find your purpose find your

# 7

## Finding Your
## Meaning and Purpose

∽

*He who has a why to live for*

*can bear almost any how.*

—FRIEDRICH NIETZSCHE

A student once asked me a very important question . . .
"What do I consider to be our purpose on this earth?"
The truth is that I haven't a clue as to what our purpose is . . .
nor, in my opinion, does anybody else. How can we know?
Our mortal minds simply cannot know the Grand Design, the
great mystery behind it all. We can speculate, but how can
we "know"?

While I admit my ignorance on the subject, I still have my
own ideas about the importance of finding our own personal
sense of purpose on this earth, and I would like to pass these
ideas on to you. They have made an enormous difference in
my life and I believe they will make a difference in yours.

For too many of us, life seems inexplicably empty. No

matter how much success we attain, or how many loving people there are in our lives, or how many activities we participate in, there still seems to be that deep yearning for something more. What is it that we are searching for? I propose that what many of us lack in our lives is that very important sense of our own purpose. Until we find it, our emptiness goes unabated.

A sense of purpose is not enough, however; it must be accompanied by a sense of meaning . . . that is, the understanding that we truly make a difference in this big, wide, wonderful world . . . that we are needed . . . that we count. I am going to make a very strong statement here: I believe that . . .

To know we really count is the most powerful and vital piece of information we can ever have.

It introduces a whole new dimension to our being—that of responsibility. Don't get scared! This kind of responsibility is not a burden. On the contrary, it enables us to leave behind the frightened ego and jump to the highest part of who we are. It allows us to create acts of love that make us feel alive and joyful, even blissful. And what is very reassuring is that our sense of meaning gives us the direction we need to take in all situations of our lives.

To spell it out more clearly:

*Our sense of meaning* is the knowledge that we truly make a difference . . . that we are needed . . .

that we are important . . . that our lives count for
something.

*Our sense of purpose* is the determination to act in
ways that are consistent with our sense of
meaning . . . that are consistent with the
knowledge that we truly do make a difference.

When a sense of meaning is combined with a sense of purpose, we have found the formula for living a wonderfully fulfilling life.

Unfortunately, not much attention is paid in our society
to the development of a sense of meaning and purpose.

- Our parents don't pay attention to it when they over-
  protect us and fail to demand that we become a contributing member of the household.

- Our schools don't pay attention to it when they fail to
  demand that we meaningfully participate in creating a
  healing and loving environment for our fellow students. (Somehow, becoming a "jock" rarely does it!)

- Our jobs don't pay attention to it when the system asks
  us to outdo others instead of working with excellence
  for the good of all concerned. Money, not meaning, is
  the bottom line.

- Society doesn't pay attention to it when it promotes
  competition instead of partnership in all aspects of

life. In competition, our sense of meaning and purpose is thwarted and we lose sight of what would give
us true joy instead of momentary applause.

Clearly, since none of the above has given us a clue, it's up to
each and every one of us to find our own sense of meaning
and purpose. And it is important that we do.

In addition to filling the emptiness within, a sense of
meaning and purpose takes away a lot of our fear about the
future, thus helping us to embrace the uncertainty. This is
because we can take our meaning and purpose with us wherever we go. It is with us in the best of times and the worst of
times. It is this sense of meaning and purpose that helps us
transcend the drama in our world and makes life worth living.

So many of my own ideas and experiences relative to this
subject derive from "logotherapy," a school of psychotherapy
created by Viktor Frankl. As you learned in the previous chapter, he was a truly remarkable man who was able to create value
even from his experience in a concentration camp. The following is one of the key incidents that helped him devise the theory that touched my life forever and hopefully will touch yours.

Frankl had a degree in medicine before he was interned
in the concentration camp. Hence, he found himself caring,
as best as he could, for a number of fellow prisoners. At one
point, he was invited to join a friend who had worked out a
plan for escaping from the camp to the freedom he so often
dreamed about. But, since Frankl was the only physician
among the prisoners, he felt uncomfortable about leaving
those who needed him. He brooded over the situation and
finally came to a remarkable conclusion. He tells us . . .

Suddenly I decided to take fate into my own hands for once. I ran out of the hut and told my friend that I could not go with him. As soon as I told him with finality that I had made up my mind to stay with my patients, the unhappy feeling left me. I did not know what the following days would bring, but I had gained an inward peace that I had never experienced before.[1]

Breathtaking! At that moment, Frankl discovered that there was something even more important than his personal freedom . . . and that was his sense of meaning and purpose. And it was just this realization that inspired him to create the school of "logotherapy," which can be translated as the psychology of meaning and purpose.*

According to logotherapy, the striving to find a meaning in one's life is the primary motivational force in a human being. That's an important realization when it comes to mental health! A great many mental conflicts, Frankl believed, are *not* a result of disease or a troubled childhood, but stem from a Spiritual distress which appears when we fail to find any kind of meaning in our lives. So, by definition, the purpose of logotherapy is to help the patient find meaning in his or her life.

Viktor Frankl has given us a precious gift. He has given us a way to rise above any negative situation in which we find ourselves. With our sense of meaning and purpose, *we can make something good out of anything bad.* Given this ability,

---

*Logos* in Greek means both meaning and spirit. Accordingly, logotherapy has a Spiritual base, not a religious base.

we don't have to get stuck in our fear of the uncertain; we can transcend to that inner place where we understand that no matter what the future brings us, our sense of meaning and purpose will help us find the gifts.

And the good news is that wherever we find ourselves, our sense of meaning and purpose is always there. All we have to do is notice! Frankl discovered his sense of meaning and purpose in a concentration camp, of all places, and it transformed him. He found a way of seeing the world that allowed him to transcend the horror of his circumstances. He found a way of standing above it all and, astonishingly, finding the blessings.

I believe that many emotional problems exist because of a lack of a sense of meaning and purpose. For example, it's a phenomenon in our culture that so many die or find themselves in a state of depression when they retire. They are filled with an inner emptiness . . . what the logotherapists would call the "the existential vacuum."

This vacuum can be there at any stage of our lives, but it often rears its ugly head when the rushing through life is over and we come face-to-face with an emptiness that was always there, but was never noticed in the frantic pace of our lives.

This emptiness is caused by the sense that our lives have no meaning. Had we developed a sense of meaning and purpose prior to our retiring, we would know that we could take that awareness with us into retirement and create value for ourselves and others in a new and wonderful way. Retirees who have a sense of meaning and purpose are enjoying life enormously.

The following quotation from the American philosopher William James beautifully describes the grand opportunity that retirement can offer all of us. And, happily, we don't have to wait for retirement to attain such a wonderful state of well-being . . .

> I am done with great things and big plans, great institutions and big success. I am for those tiny, invisible loving human forces that work from individual to individual, creeping through the crannies of the world like so many rootlets, or like the capillary oozing of water, which, if given time, will rend the hardest monuments of pride.

Gorgeous! I am a great people-watcher, and it hasn't escaped my vision that people yearn for meaning, and yet what they think they need is success in the material sense. Unfulfilled, many kill themselves with alcohol, drugs, greed, and sometimes suicide. Understand that there is nothing wrong with success in the material sense PLUS a sense of meaning and purpose. But without the latter, we are lost.

The implications of having a sense of meaning and purpose are enormous. Think about it. A sense of meaning and purpose puts us powerfully in the role of "giver" rather than "getter." As Viktor Frankl learned . . .

> It did not really matter what we expected from life, but rather what life expected from us.

Eric Clapton made this discovery in his own way. I once heard him say that so much of his life didn't turn out the way he wanted. But he has learned that . . .

It's not about what I want my life to be, it's about what I can give.

And giving he is. Aside from giving us his wonderful music, he has created the Crossroads Centre in Antigua, a small island in the eastern Caribbean. Crossroads Centre is a treatment center for alcohol and drug addiction for people from around the world. As to why he is so involved, he says, "I had treatment and I want to give something back."[2] Do you see the magnificence here? He suffered greatly, *but through his suffering* he was able to find a sense of meaning and purpose. To find meaning in the suffering is about as Spiritually high as we can get.

That puts an awesomely different twist on life, doesn't it? Most of us focus on what we want life to give us. In fact, it is just this kind of thinking that creates the victim mentality that is sweeping our society today. The victim mentality is self-destructive as it says rather pathetically, "Poor me. I'm not getting what I want." We need to learn that when we play the role of victim, we give away all our power. When, instead, we play the role of a person who has meaning and purpose in this world, our power is unlimited. And we act in wonderful ways that restore and enhance our sense of self.

We all need to determine for ourselves which specific

actions to take that emanate directly from our sense of meaning and purpose. This determination gives us peace about the uncertainty in our lives. For example, if you know that you have meaning and decide that your purpose is to radiate love, does it really matter where or how you do this? If you lose your job, you can still radiate love. If you lose your loved one, you can still radiate love. If you have a chronic ailment, you can still radiate love. This important dynamic explains the magnificent actions and reactions of the beautiful souls I talked about in the previous chapter and so many others who have used their difficulties in life to help others. *The story is just the drama, the meaning and purpose help us rise above the drama.*

"Okay, Susan. You've convinced us. How do we find a sense of meaning and purpose?" You don't ask me easy questions, do you? I'm sure there are many avenues I haven't even thought about, but let me offer you some very effective exercises to move you in the right direction. And then, I trust, you'll take it from there!

## THE "WHAT AM I ASKED TO DO?" EXERCISE

Since we are all part of the Grand Design, cosmically speaking, I believe each of us is asked as a human being to do something to help this world. How do we find what it is that we are asked to do? I once heard it said . . .

Stand where you are, make a circle, see what needs to be done and do it.

Using myself as an example, I made a circle, metaphorically speaking, and I saw that I was called upon to learn and teach . . . specifically, I was called upon to learn how to see the world through the eyes of the Higher Self and share what I learned with others. So I now spend my time learning about living in the Higher Self so that I have something valuable to teach. In this way, all of my life experiences are "grist for the mill." Whether my experiences are good or bad, they all have inherent value that I can pass on to others. As I mentioned earlier, my breast cancer was a valuable experience, as it gave me the opportunity to help others with their fears about breast cancer. You get the point.

As you make your own circle and look for what needs to be done, it helps to look at what you *love* to do. Our personal interests are so often tuned in to the Grand Design. Therefore, these personal interests often send us in the right direction as to how to fulfill our sense of meaning and purpose. The questions then become . . .

What do I love to do? How do I use what I love to do
to help the world around me?

If you love to cook, you can put nourishment into this world. You can feed your family and friends. You can create a restaurant that brings people pleasure. You can help in a soup kitchen feeding the poor. Or all of the above. If you love being around children, you can put nurturing into the world as a teacher, mentor, and/or parent. If you love gardening, you can put beauty into the world everywhere you go and with all the people you meet. If your answer is developing new technology, you could put wonderful energy into the world by finding ways of enriching it instead of destroying it. No matter what you love to do, there is no end to what you can do to help people near and far.

It is important to keep in mind that what we are asked to do changes with our circumstances in life. It would be unwise to hang on to any particular means of spreading our meaning and purpose into this world. There is always something wonderful to do in whatever form that takes.

There are also things we are ALL asked to do in the course of everyday living. When we have a sense of meaning and purpose, we don't litter, we keep the noise down in our homes so as not to bother the neighbors, we volunteer, we make others feel comfortable, and so on. You get the picture. We become thinking, loving individuals who care about the feelings of others and act accordingly. Trust me when I tell you that . . .

When you see people who act irresponsibly and uncaringly to the people around them, you can be sure that they have no sense of meaning and purpose.

Motivational speaker Zig Ziglar showed great wisdom when he noted that "every obnoxious act is a cry for help." I believe that is true. This may help us have compassion for the less enlightened among us.

You might be wondering, "How do I know if the purpose I choose is the right one?" Don Juan, a Yaqui warrior, told his student Carlos Castaneda the following, and it warms the heart and sends you in the perfect direction:

> Does this path have a heart? If it does, the path is good; if it doesn't, it is of no use. Both paths lead nowhere; but one has a heart; the other doesn't. One makes for a joyful journey; as long as you follow it, you are one with it. The other will make you curse your life. One makes you strong; the other weakens you.[3]

I always know when I am off track relative to my life purpose. I lose my sense of enjoyment. When I'm once again on my self-created "path with the heart," the joy returns. I stop worrying about the petty things that drive me crazy and I am at peace once again.

By the way, the phrase that intrigues me in the above quotation from Don Juan is, "Both paths lead nowhere." What does that mean? I can think of a number of interpretations, but I like the one that suggests to me we are all traveling this same Journey through life together. But how we choose to be on that Journey is up to us. Do we want to be miserable or do we want to be happy? When we follow the path with the heart, happiness comes right along with us. That's just the way it is.

The very good news is that no matter what stage of life we are in . . . whether we are in school, raising a family, working, retired, or whatever . . . there is always a purpose to be fulfilled. We never outlive our usefulness. As our children leave the house to create their own lives, as we retire from a life of working, as we become one of the wise elders, there is always someone or something in this world that absolutely needs us in some special way. Our task is simply to look around and find that someone or something and step right in. *There is never a time when there is nothing for us to do.*

Let me remind you of the beautiful story I brought to you in *Feel the Fear and Do It Anyway.* A woman in New York was bedridden after leading a very active life. She asked herself, "How can I be of help when I can't even get out of bed?" She found an answer. She obtained the phone numbers of others who were bedridden and made it her "job" to call them daily just to let them know that someone cared. She made many phone pals and brought much joy to others.

Some of us have the opposite problem. Instead of feeling we have nothing to do, we feel there is too much to do! We are busy, busy, busy, creating money, following the "rules" of raising our children instead of trusting our gut, and often taking all the riches in our lives for granted. What we may NOT be busy doing is noticing how important we are to those around us. Because of this, we totally miss the rewards of a life well lived and, in fact, we often feel resentful.

As we pay attention to the fact that our lives have meaning and purpose, however, our efforts seem worthwhile and we are grateful for the opportunity to play such an important part in it all.

So make your circle, see what needs to be done, and do it—with excellence, integrity, pride, and gratitude that you truly are making a difference in this world. For you truly are.

## THE "ACT-AS-IF" EXERCISE

You may still not have the understanding at the deepest level of your being that your life actually does make a difference in this world. You may act lovingly and do wonderful things, but you still don't feel you are important. You can begin to change this erroneous self-perception by playing the game of "act-as-if." That is, with each step of the Journey you ask yourself . . .

"If I truly made a difference in this world, what
would I be doing?"
"If I truly made a difference in this world, how
would I be more loving?"
"If I truly made a difference in this world, how
would I create more harmony around me?"

You then make a list of all the actions you would take in all situations in your life. And then you would act accordingly. For example:

If I truly made a difference in this world, what would I be doing relative to my job? How could I be more loving and create more harmony around me?

1. I would arrive on time.
2. I would be a self-starter, advancing the goals of my company.
3. I would be friendly to my co-workers.
4. I would give them credit when they do something meaningful.

And so on. And then you would follow through on these "I would's." The above answers are rather ordinary and obvious, but I am putting my trust in you to be much more creative in your own personal situation. The challenge is to create a wonderful environment for yourself and everyone around you. It doesn't matter at what level of the company you function—from the lowest on the totem pole to the highest. Your sense of caring is important no matter where you find yourself.

You need to play this game of act-as-if in all areas of your life . . . with your family, friends, career, and community And don't forget to include giving love and caring to yourself. Without yourself, you can't do much of anything!

As you can see, the process is very simple, but it requires a lifetime commitment of asking yourself these important questions, listening for the answers that come from the highest part of who you are, and then taking the actions that create a healing energy within and around you. The challenge is to ask yourself these questions in all the circumstances in your life . . .

> if you lose your job,
> if you get a promotion,
> if you become ill,
> if you are healthy,
> if you work,
> if you are walking down the street,
> if you are driving you car,
> if you lose a loved one,
> if you are happy,

if you are sad,
if you are shopping,
if you lose money in the stock market,
if you gain money in the stock market,
if your partner leaves,
if your partner stays,
if . . .

And then let your actions flow from the answers you get. Now here's the good news:

As we consciously and patiently use this life-giving game of "act-as-if," we ultimately *live into* the awesome understanding of just how large a difference we can truly make.

We learn that, whether in the enclosed space of our home or out in the vastness of the world, every action we take helps determine whether this is a world filled with hate and conflict or a world filled with peace and love.

Along the way, we may notice that the lingering anger and pain of past and present hurts can make positive actions difficult. Whenever our hearts are filled with anger and pain, it is difficult, if not impossible, to spread an energy of peace and love onto this earth. At such times, it is empowering to pick up the mirror instead of the magnifying glass and ask ourselves . . .

"How can I heal the hurt within?" "How can I change what doesn't work in my life?" "How can I transcend to that place where all is love?"

And once again, we look to our Higher Self to find the answers. It is a bit like filling in the pieces of a jigsaw puzzle with many "Aha's" along the way. Looked at it in this way, life becomes an exciting journey of discovery instead of a series of hurtful events that make us miserable.

You won't get it right all the time, but more and more you will find the joy of being a source of love and caring. You can speed the process by affirming many times throughout each day . . .

I am a powerful and loving person who has so much to give to this world. I bring love and peace wherever I go.

Whether you believe these words or not, their repetition brings forth the powerful and loving energy that you hold within.

I can assure you that if you act-as-if long enough, the magnificence of who you are will ultimately be clear to you. That is the day you will cry tears of joy at this profound new sense of yourself. Certainly that was my experience many years ago when it dawned on me that my life made a difference. I trust that it will be your experience as well.

---

## THE "FIND MEANING
## IN THE SUFFERING" EXERCISE

There is no question that life includes both joy and suffering. As you have already learned, our suffering is lessened when we can find the meaning and purpose in it all. Each of the heroes in the previous chapter found meaning in the "unthinkable" happenings in their lives and, in that, their suffering became a valuable gift.

I'm sure you can think of many other "heroes" who, from their suffering, have been able to give us the assurance that, "Hey, it's okay. No matter what happens, you can find the good." What a gift they give us! When we can find meaning in the suffering, we survive it all with a sense of gratitude rather than upset.

This doesn't mean that when bad times occur there aren't times of intense pain, fear, and upset. At such times, we are wise to enter the wonderful Land of Tears that I mentioned in a previous chapter.[4] But at some point, we say to ourselves, "Okay, enough pain. Let's see how I can use this experience to create a better world out there, for myself and everyone around me."

All of us "suffer" in a multitude of ways, including, migraines, financial problems, difficult children, loss of people we love, illness, and so on. I venture to say that no matter how bad things may seem, we can ultimately make something positive out of whatever happens to us.

So your task in this exercise is to . . .

1) Make a list of all that is going wrong in your life, all that is causing you to suffer, and determine that you will find a way to find the blessings. And then . . .
2) Look for ways in which you can express your meaning and purpose through the suffering. You will find many ways of doing this.

It is important to *pay attention* to what life is giving you through any suffering you are experiencing. If you don't pay attention, you will miss the opportunity in it all; if you do pay attention, you will see all the gifts that are there to enrich your life and the lives of so many others.

---

## THE "TEACH THE CHILDREN" EXERCISE

If you think about children in today's Western world, it is obvious that so many of them have not been given a sense of meaning and purpose. This is evidenced by increased violence, rudeness, lack of caring, lack of a sense of responsibility, depression, and even suicide. I believe that *very little of this kind of behavior would occur if children understood that they made a difference.* So how do we teach them that they are important and that they have meaning and purpose in this world?

Let me answer this by sharing with you an article I wrote for my website some time ago. It would be world-changing if the message in this article could start a chain of events leading to loving actions by our children. Here's the article:

"A friend of mine, Karen, was asked by her seventeen-year-old stepson, Jeff, if she could think of anything special he could do with his girlfriend on Valentine's Day, that is, in addition to the traditional romantic dinner. Karen thought for a moment and said, "Why don't you go down to the supermarket and buy fifty roses? Then go to a home for the elderly and give everyone there a rose. That would be a very loving thing to do. And the roses at the supermarket are on sale right now." Jeff wasn't expecting this kind of a suggestion, but much to his credit, he decided to do it.

Karen then called one of the homes for the elderly in the surrounding area and asked if it would be all right for Jeff to come by with his girlfriend and pass around the roses. The nurse who picked up the phone was more than enthusiastic; she was ecstatic! "No one has ever done anything like this in the past," she said, "and it would make such a difference to the people here."

Jeff and his girlfriend showed up at the appointed hour a little nervous, not knowing what to expect. But they soon got into the swing of things as they went around the home for the elderly passing out the roses, smiling, talking, and giving everyone there the feeling that somebody cared. Jeff came back home thrilled at how welcoming everyone was and how good it made him feel. When Karen told me this story, I was so moved that I cried! I also noted that Jeff's girlfriend must have fallen in love with him for life!

I believe that my friend, Karen, has come up with the cure for so many of the ills with our children in today's world. So few young people are called upon to help those around them. Our society focuses on the importance of winning which is very alienating; it doesn't focus on the importance of giving which is very loving. As a result, we are left with an abundance of self-absorbed "brats" who don't realize that their lives make a difference. Perhaps the greatest thing we can teach our children is that they DO make a difference. The only way they can learn this important fact is by being exposed to ways in which they can give to the world around them. I might add that we need to congratulate Jeff on his willingness to do something that was so different from traditional expectations on Valentine's Day.

As Karen told me her story, I remembered back to a story one of my workshop attendees, Melanie, told me. It was Christmas and, after opening a multitude of presents, all her six-year-old daughter had to say was, "Is that all?" Exasperated, Melanie came up with a plan that worked miracles. Starting the following January, she and her daughter began making gifts, which they would distribute to patients in a local hospital the following Christmas. As the months passed, her daughter got more and more excited about the approaching Christmas . . . not because of what she was going to GET, but because of what she was going to GIVE. Powerful!

My children were lucky. For the ten years that I worked at the Floating Hospital, they were exposed to the joy of giving as they volunteered to help whenever they could. To this day, they are involved with various projects to help the poor and to save the environment. I applaud them for caring so much. My daughter says that whenever she feels bad about anything in her life, the solution is easy. She gets herself out of the house and finds a way to help others. It works all the time to make her realize how important her life is to others in this world. Beautiful!

The implication of all I have told you is so simple. It is so obvious. Yet it is overlooked. The way we build self-esteem in our children is to teach them to act in ways that build self-esteem! Telling children repeatedly how wonderful they are doesn't make them feel wonderful about themselves. *Showing them how to act in a way that helps the world around them does make them feel wonderful about themselves.* Perhaps this is a good lesson for all of us adults as well.

I received some wonderful feedback from this article. It pointed out to many that from a very early age, *we need to expect more from our children.* Children are mollycoddled beyond what is healthy in our over-the-top, child-centered world. We also need to lessen our emphasis on the importance of competition and increase our emphasis on the importance and the joy of helping others. We also need to emphasize the beauty of their acts of giving, instead of only focusing on their weaknesses. As to this last point, I was pleased to discover a wonderful example of an organization doing just this.

The International Youth Hall of Fame has found a way of rewarding children who are doing good things for their community. This is done in a way that just keeps giving and giving and giving. Children are "secretly" nominated so as to avoid their competing to win. Nominees then *choose* if they want to be honored by publicly taking a pledge to mentor and encourage another young person and then partner with them in a community service project. When the project is completed, they become official honorees and are able to create a personal message in pictures and/or words that is etched into eight-inch ceramic tiles. These tiles are used to construct Youth Walls of Fame, thus assuring that these young people leave an important legacy for future generations.

Whether you have children or not, put on your thinking caps and consider how we can all create programs to give children a sense of meaning and purpose. It is very clear to me that . . .

We must stop shielding children from the strength, love, and meaning that they all embody.

Yes, shockingly, that is what we do when we give them everything and expect nothing in return. That is what we do when we ask them only to compete with each other in an unhealthy win-at-any-cost way and neglect to teach them that they make a difference in terms of making this a more loving world.

And, if we feel competition is so important for our children (which many people seem to feel), why don't we have them competing to be the most giving? I agree that getting a ball into a hoop may have some value in a healthy competitive environment, but I don't believe that it builds a sense of self as effectively as feeding the poor, or reading to the blind, or mentoring those who are younger. You get the picture.

It's such a delicious opportunity when you think about

it . . . teaching children that they truly count . . . that they make a difference in this world . . . that their life matters for something. And then giving them the most important opportunity that education can provide—the opportunity for them to find ways of helping the world in their own special way.

## THE "GIVE YOURSELF AWAY" EXERCISE

As I suggested earlier, a happy life isn't about getting what you want in a material sense. It's about giving what you've got in any form that takes. We recently had the opportunity to watch so many people give themselves away. And I speak of the many acts of supreme generosity that occurred after the terrorist attacks in New York and Washington.

Young and old "gave themselves away" as they got involved in the task of helping. Young kids with their lemonade stands, entertainers, businessmen, sports figures, the medical establishment, and the ordinary people who became extraordinary as they gave of themselves to raise money and help those in need. And as I mentioned in Chapter 5, we witnessed the firemen, policemen, and volunteers risking—and sometimes losing—their lives to rescue others. Some beautiful beings actually sacrificed their lives rather than leaving others—sometimes total strangers—to die alone in the towering buildings that soon became rubble.

Thankfully such dramatic events do not usually dominate our lives, but we still have the opportunity to give ourselves away in the course of our everyday experiences. Let me give you a little practice in using that wonderful giving part of yourself. Remember the focus is not "I'll do this to make myself happy." Rather, "I'll do this because I can make someone else happy." Try the following and see what happens:

I talked about those fifty roses in the previous exercise. Symbolically, I am giving you fifty roses right now. I ask you,

"Who are you going to give your roses to?"

And then I want you to give them away in the form of loving actions. Keep a list of the things you are doing for others until you reach the number fifty. I'll then give you another fifty roses. Actually, you won't need me any longer to spur you on. You will feel so good noticing the joy you bring to others that you will find enough roses to give away for the rest of your life.

To me, the roses symbolize an awakening in the self to the needs of others, the pain of others, the hopes of others, the feelings of others. One rose opens a heart . . . not only someone else's heart, but your own as well. Giving your fifty roses is becoming involved. It's becoming part of the dream. It's leaving behind the frightened ego and jumping to the part of yourself where you truly know you make a difference. It's about ending the yearning and fulfilling the promise of who you are as a human being.

So begin giving those fifty roses away. You never have to worry if roses are in season or not. Love is always in season. And once you start planting love, the garden just grows and grows and grows. Magnificent!

live joyously live joyously live joyously live joyously
live joyously live joyously live joyously live joyously
live joyously live joyously live joyously live joyously
live joyously live joyously live joyously live joyously
live joyously live joyously live joyously live joyously
live joyously live joyously **live joyously** live joyously
live joyously live joyously live joyously live joyously
live joyously live joyously live joyously live joyously
live joyously live joyously live joyously live joyously
live joyously live joyously live joyously live joyously
live joyously live joyously live joyously live joyously
live joyously live joyously live joyously live joyously
live joyously **live joyously** live joyously live joyously
live joyously live joyously live joyously live joyously
live joyously live joyously live joyously live joyously
live joyously live joyously live joyously live joyously
live joyously live joyously live joyously live joyously
live joyously live joyously live joyously live joyously
live joyously live joyously live joyously live joyously
**live joyously** live joyously live joyously live joyously
live joyously live joyously live joyously live joyously
live joyously live joyously live joyously live joyously
live joyously live joyously live joyously live joyously
live joyously live joyously live joyously live joyously
live joyously live joyously live joyously live joyously
live joyously live joyously live joyously live joyously
live joyously live joyously live joyously live joyously
live joyously live joyously live joyously live joyously
live joyously live joyously live joyously **live joyously**

# 8

# Embracing the
# Ultimate Uncertainty

∞

*No man knows whether death, which men in*
*their fear apprehend to be the greatest evil,*
*may not be the greatest good.*

—SOCRATES[1]

Yes, this is a chapter about death. "But, Susan, I don't
want to read about death!" I'm sure many of you have an
aversion to this seemingly dark subject, but how could I write
a book about uncertainty without looking at the subject of
death? After all, what can be more uncertain than that? That
is to say, while we are certain that we will die, we couldn't be
more uncertain as to what death is all about.

Don't you think it is strange that human beings look away
from something that happens to each and every one of us?
No one is excluded. I would think we would want to jump
right in and learn as much as we possibly can about the dying
process. If we did, we would discover that it is possible to
anticipate our own death and even the death of those we love

with some sadness, of course, but with also a serene sense of wonder and peace.

Actually, we unwisely think of death as something to dread. As a result, most of us would prefer not to think about it at all, especially when we are young and vibrant and looking forward to a long, long life ahead of us. But whether we are young or old, it would indeed serve us well to "embrace the hearse."*

How do I define "embracing the hearse"? I define it as "being totally at peace with the prospect of death while joyously living each day to the fullest." And a quotation from John De La Fontaine adds another important dimension. He said . . .

Death never takes the wise man by surprise. He is always ready to go.[2]

Yes, embracing the hearse is also being ready to go. "But, Susan, how can anyone be ready to go?" That's a very good question, one I've thought a lot about myself. While it could be the subject of an entire LARGE book, let me give you just a few thoughts and exercises to set you on the path toward greater acceptance of something we and all our loved ones will experience sooner or later.

---

*This wonderful phrase comes "accidentally" from a French student of Chungliang Al Huang as he explains in his wonderful book *Quantum Soup: Fortune Cookies in Danger*, Celestial Arts, Berkeley, CA, 1991, p. 130. The student meant to say "Embrace the Horse" and ended up saying "Embrace the Hearse." A wise mistake, indeed!

## THE "JUMP RIGHT IN" EXERCISE

One of the ways we can "get ready to go," whether we are eight or eighty years old, is not to avoid looking at death, but rather to jump right in and keep it in view at all times, not as a *morbid preoccupation*, but as a reminder to live life NOW rather than putting it off until some later date that may—or may not—come. Here are a few suggestions as to how to jump right in:

1a) I was once told that certain Spiritual masters in Tibet used to set their teacups upside down before they went to bed each night as a reminder that life was impermanent. And then, when they awoke each morning, they turned their teacups right side up again with the happy thought, "I'm still here!" This simple gesture was a wonderful reminder to celebrate every moment of the day.

Certainly we all need reminders that we are privileged to be alive, that life is short, and we need to make the most of it. Unfortunately, most of us wake up leaving the teacup upside down, metaphorically speaking, dragging through the day, putting off life, thinking we will live forever but acting if we were already dead! "No joy today. Another time perhaps."

I suggest you take a page from the instruction book of the Tibetan masters and have your own teacup ritual. Place a teacup and saucer by your bedside. Then, do as the Tibetan masters did and actually turn your teacup over each night before you go to bed. And when you awake, put it right side up once again with thanks in your heart for the gift of life.

We need constant reminders that life is short and we need to appreciate every moment we have.

1b) Another easy way of jumping right in is to reinstate a simple little prayer from our childhood that I'll bet many of you have forgotten about. This prayer allows us to stop worrying and, instead, turn our fate over to a Higher Power. It goes like this . . .

> Now I lay me down to sleep.
> I pray the Lord my Soul to keep.
> If I should die before I wake,
> I pray the Lord my Soul to take.

While I personally love this prayer, there are those who have told me that it frightened them as a young child and they shudder when they hear it. Given this, one can argue that maybe it shouldn't be used as a prayer for children!* But I see it as a wonderful prayer for adults who perhaps are better able to handle the realities of life and death. It's a real "let go" kind of prayer that holds no fear or any expectations of living forever. It peacefully acknowledges that death is always a possibility. Whether we are healthy, sick, young, or old, this lovely prayer says that we are ready to go.

---

*If this prayer affects you negatively, you can always find another prayer to give you peace of mind. See "The Perfect Prayer Exercise" on page 222.

EMBRACING THE ULTIMATE UNCERTAINTY | 167

You may not believe in "the Lord" or any other kind of Higher Power, for that matter. Not to worry. It is irrelevant whether you believe in a Higher Power or not. It's a prayer that simply says, "Universe, take over" and you can interpret the term Universe in the way that is most comfortable for you.

So as you are going off to bed, you can repeat this little prayer over and over again until it becomes automatic in your mind. In so doing, you will feel a sense of peace and trust as you fall asleep. And when you awake the following day, awake with gratitude for one more beautiful day of life.

2) A much more dramatic and participatory way you can jump right in is to be around people who are dying. (Of course, we'll ALL die eventually, but you know what I mean!) You will learn so much. One of the things you will learn is that while many are afraid to die, many are not. In fact, there are many who are very ready to go when their time comes. They don't resist death, they welcome it, they learn from it, they are at peace with it. Some even joke about it.

One of my heroes relative to the dying process is Rob Eichburg who, a number of years ago, died from complications related to AIDS. He was the author of a book entitled *Coming Out: An Act of Love*, which helped many people handle the difficulties in life as a result of being homosexual. When news of his impending death spread, his answering machine was filled with messages from people giving him their thanks for all he had done to improve their lives. This gave him great comfort.

Mark and I "jumped right in" and spent a lot of time with

Rob, especially during the last two weeks of his life. While we initially felt that spending time with someone who was so young and so ill would be very difficult for us, we ended up treasuring every moment. We went there to help Rob, but in so many ways, he helped us. As he was dying, there was, yes, sadness, as he felt he had so much more to contribute to this world, but also joy that he had lived a rich, full life. There was also a great deal of humor and healing.

For example, he asked me to help him "let go," as he was definitely a control freak. During one of our conversations, he was obsessing about some minor details relative to the plans his mother was making for his funeral.* In a very level and firm voice and with a very straight face, I said, "Rob, you're not letting go." We both burst out laughing at the realization that, even after his death, he wanted to control everything!

The day before Rob died, my husband and I had to go out of town for a few weeks. Before we left, we went to say good-bye to Rob. As we were leaving his bedroom, he said, "Have a great trip." I looked him in the eyes, realizing that the end was very near for him and that I probably would not see him again. I said softly and lovingly, "You have a great trip, too, Rob." It was a very poignant and beautiful moment, which we both captured. And then came a response that was filled with his wonderful courage and humor. "If I'm still here when you get back, I'll really be pissed!" And once again the air was filled with laughter.

---

*Rob's mother, Shirley, is a loving, strong woman who was able to go through the experience of Rob's "control freak" behavior and his ultimate death with her own sense of dignity and humor. She is an inspiration to us all.

That was my last memory of Rob alive . . . laughing, accepting, and loving. I'm sure that Rob faced a lot of painful feelings, including fear, before he got to that wonderful state of acceptance, but certainly at the time of his death, he was very ready to "embrace the hearse."

The fact that we can find so many who have found enrichment in the dying process should give us all a sense of freedom in the prospects of our own death or even of the death of those we love.

To help you experience firsthand that there can be beauty in the dying process, you may want to volunteer to help in an organization, such as a hospice, that cares for the dying. There you can find an incredible opportunity for Spiritual growth. It is an amazing feeling to touch with love what we normally touch with fear. There are many terminally ill people who can teach us that even with the pain . . .

We can heal the soul even though the body cannot be healed . . . we can be at peace . . . we can laugh . . . we can feel blessed . . . we can be free of emotional pain . . . we can look forward to the next big adventure.

So all is not lost when we or our loved ones face death. In fact, as we can learn how to "embrace the hearse," there is so much to be gained.

## THE "WHAT'S NEXT" EXERCISE

A deep Spirituality certainly helps us all transcend the fear of death. For example, when we feel that the essence of who we are is not our body, but a transcendent Spirit, we feel as if death doesn't take the totality of who we are. The best of us is free to go on. I love the observation of John Quincy Adams the sixth president of the United States, three days before he died way back in 1848. He said . . .

John Quincy Adams is well, but the house in which he lives at the present time is becoming dilapidated. It's tottering on its foundations. Time and the seasons have nearly destroyed it. Its roof is pretty well worn out. Its walls are shattered and tremble with every wind. I think John Quincy Adams will have to move out of it pretty soon. But he, himself, is quite well, thank you.[3]

John Quincy Adams is saying that his body only holds who he is temporarily. And that he will soon be changing his address. That's a very comforting way to view death.

Ram Dass, one of my "heroes" in Chapter 6, often talks about Emmanuel, a disembodied Spirit that speaks "through" Pat Rodegast. Ram Dass told Emmanuel that he ministers to people who are dying, and asked if there was anything he could tell them to ease their minds. Emmanuel replied, "Ram Dass, tell them that death is *absolutely* safe. It's like taking off a tight shoe."[4] What a great image. Seeing death as freedom in the most comfortable sense!

The people who wrote the dictionary have nothing reassuring to tell us about death. They define it as "the end of life." How do they know that? It is unfortunate that they forgot to add that powerful word . . . MAYBE. In truth, we don't really know what happens to the Spirit when a person leaves his or her body. We do have some clues, however, that it does go on to another dimension of being. These clues come from those who have actually "come back" from death. Let me tell you a little about near-death experiences or NDEs for short.

Many books have been written about NDEs. They are defined as *the experiences of those who have been pronounced "clinically dead," yet have come back to life*. Many return with astonishing and enlightening tales to tell. While a small number say it was a bad experience and they couldn't wait to return to their bodies, the great majority reported that the experience is sublime.

While no two NDEs are identical, there seem to be some striking similarities. Most report experiencing one or more of the following . . .

- A tunnel and/or a radiant light.

- A great resistance to coming back to life. In the state of being clinically dead, they find a sense of overwhelming peace, love, painlessness, joy, and a sense of being part of the entire Universe.

- Many reported returning to life with great reluctance after they were given the message that it wasn't their time to go. They would have preferred to go forward into the light. Others reported that they returned only because they felt they still had too much to do here on earth, such as raising their children. But the experience totally took away their fear of dying, whenever their time may come.

One would like to imagine, given the above, that those who actually did complete the dying process moved forward into a sublime place of peace and love.

- Some surgical patients reported floating out of their body while in a clinically dead state. Hospital personnel were astounded when their patients described events taking place while they were clinically dead *that could only be known if they were "above" the situation looking down.* Astounding!

- When they return to life, most who have experienced NDEs are more compassionate, giving, and optimistic. They are less focused on material things. They experience better health and less stress. They have a better sense of humor and lightness. And they certainly lose their fear of death!

- Interestingly, even children who have been declared clinically dead report the same findings as adults. Dr. Melvin Morse, a pediatrician who interviewed hundreds of children who had been declared clinically dead, reports that the children told him over and over again in their own words that the end of life as we know it is serene and joyful and not to be feared.[5] He believes that the reported experiences of children are very trustworthy as, with their limited knowledge, children are less biased than adults. This information should be a great comfort to those who have lost their beloved children.

And I could go on. More and more research is being conducted on NDEs. In fact, there is an association devoted entirely to them. It is called the International Association for Near-Death Studies (IANDS) at the University of Connecticut.[6] You may want to investigate further

All the research I looked at tells me that NDEs are unaffected by a person's culture, religion, race, belief system, age, or seemingly anything else. They can happen to anyone, religious or not, and whether one believes in God or not. IANDS reports that a 1982 Gallup poll estimated that roughly 8 million adults in the United States alone have experienced an NDE. That's not counting children or those who think it's too "strange" to talk about. All the evidence collected from those who experienced NDEs should give us pause if we think of death as a terrible thing. It could be magnificent beyond words.

Of course, there are the skeptics who think that NDEs are all hogwash. Maybe they're right and maybe they're wrong. I prefer to trust that there is something out there that is sublime beyond our human ability to comprehend. As Spiritual counselor Hugh Prather tells us . . .

Why choose to be right instead of happy when there is no way to be right?[7]

Good question! Certainly the knowledge of NDEs can ease our minds about the uncertainty of dying and take away some of the pain of losing those we love. The thought that when we die we enter a place of peace, love, and all good things is very comforting, indeed.

I might add that while I have never experienced an NDE, I certainly have had "peak experiences" that are very similar to the descriptions of NDEs. There have been certain times when standing alone at the edge of the ocean or overlooking a magnificent view that I have had the similar experience of "melting" into this Universal Light. In this beautiful space, I experienced an indescribable sense of peace and safety. These experiences suggest to me that there definitely *is* something more than meets the eye and that we all have so much to look forward to in life . . . and beyond.

---

## THE "I HAVE HAD THIS" EXERCISE

Many of us fear the prospect of dying because we feel that life is passing us by and we haven't as yet lived. Who wants to die before they have lived? Not me! And not you! To give me the realization that life is not passing me by, I have made it my practice to say to myself when experiencing the simplest of life's joy, "I have had this." What this means to me is, "Life is NOT passing me by. I have enjoyed this. I have experienced this. I HAVE HAD THIS." For example . . .

When taking a walk on a magnificent day, I stop for a moment while enjoying the view and say to myself,

"I have had this."

When enjoying a meal with my wonderful husband, I say to myself, "I have had this."

When taking in the delicious warmth of the fire in my fireplace, I say to myself, "I have had this."

When leaving the cinema after seeing a beautiful movie, I say to myself, "I have had this."

When spending a day with my loving family, I say to myself, "I have had this."

As I collect my "I have had this" experiences, I fill myself with the joy of a life well lived. And my fear of death is greatly diminished. I live with the thought, "If I die tomorrow, I have had all these wonderful experiences."

So your assignment now is to begin collecting "I have had this" experiences. As you start paying attention to all the wonderful moments of you life, just keep saying to yourself, "I have had this." Whatever the event . . . a moment of success in your job, a moment of joy you get from giving to another human being, a moment of togetherness with those you love, a moment of experiencing the beauty of nature, or whatever it is for you . . . just say to yourself, "I have had this." And really take in the beauty of the moment.

You may want to create an "I have had this" jar. Write down all of your "I have had this" experiences on little slips of paper and put them in a clear glass jar to remind you. As you watch those "I have had this" experiences accumulate into the feeling of a life well lived, you will learn that life is not passing you by at all. You are walking right along with life and gathering all that it has to offer. You're not missing a thing!

## THE "DO IT NOW" EXERCISE

If you live to be 150, life is still short. As I said earlier, it is important to make the prospect of death a wonderful reminder to live NOW. So many of us put off doing the things we really want to do in life, whether these things have to do with career, play, travel, friends, relationship, children, contribution to this big, wide, wonderful world, or whatever it is for you. Our excuse is that we'll do it all later . . . when we have more time. But time goes by . . . and we still never seem to have enough time! Ultimately, some of us even forget what it was that we wanted to do in the first place.

Well, we all know that the future is uncertain; therefore it's time we figured out what we wanted to do in life and begin doing it right NOW, not later! This means . . .

Make a list with the heading "THIS IS WHAT I WANT TO EXPERIENCE IN MY LIFETIME" and GO FOR IT . . . BEGINNING RIGHT NOW!

I don't care if you are young or old; your task right now is to start making room in your life for those things you truly want to do. Yes, we all have certain responsibilities in our life, and they differ for everyone. But, even with our responsibilities, we can attend to our own needs to live life NOW!

This is one assignment I'll certainly be doing right along with you. My work is always my excuse for not doing other things that I love to do . . . like dancing, or spending more time with friends and family, like relaxing more and reading frivolous mystery novels, like taking days just to play. I'm sure that many of you can relate to that. (I'll talk more about this important subject in the following chapter.)

Right now, it's time for me and it's time for you to change our habit of putting off our dreams and desires until later. I ask you, "WHAT ARE WE WAITING FOR?"

## THE "HAPPY FUNERAL" EXERCISE

"A happy funeral, Susan? What are you talking about?" I have been to a number of funerals and it is fascinating to me how differently people plan and experience them. Some funerals are morbid and depressing; some are joyous, light, and filled with a sense of a life well lived.

My sister and I chose to make our mother's funeral joyous and light. Much to the surprise of the funeral director and the folks in the little town in which we grew up, we celebrated our mother's life and kept an air of lightness and fun throughout the ceremony. I gave a loving and humorous talk that had all her friends laughing in sweet remembrance. I think everyone went home happier than when they came in . . . and that is good. They were so used to somber and death-filled services instead of ones that were life-filled.

Subsequently, I have been to a number of "happy funerals." They included sadness and tears, of course, but they were also filled with joy in the form of endearing stories, laughter, thanks, memories of a life well lived . . . and even balloons to send the loved one on his or her way. Of course, we all have to go through the process of grief when a loved one dies. It is healing to do so. But a funeral can truly be an event of joyous remembrance and a glorious send-off as the Soul of someone we love enters a new dimension of being.

Keep a "happy funeral" in mind if you find yourself having to plan a funeral for someone you love. Also, you might want to jump right into the spirit of things and decide what you want your own funeral to be like. Then make sure you let your loved ones know. You can say something like this . . .

"When I die, I would like it to be the best party I ever attended. I plan to be there in spirit and I expect to have a great time! I want to hear laughter, and compliments, and see color everywhere . . . absolutely no black allowed, and lots of balloons."

Certainly that's what I told the people I love . . . and I expect them to honor my request!

## THE "THANK THEM NOW" EXERCISE

There are so many things we need to complete before we feel at peace with the prospect of our own death or the death of those we love. One of the most important things we need to do is to heal the hurts and say thank you to significant people in our lives. When my father died suddenly at the young age of fifty-three, I was emotionally devastated. What made the loss particularly upsetting to me was the sense that I had not told him how much I loved him and how much I appreciated all that he had given me throughout my life. I wanted him to know how I felt and at the time it seemed that it was too late.*

I learned my lesson, however. My mother was still alive, and I didn't want to make the same mistake. So after my father's death, I began repeatedly expressing my thanks to my mother and letting her know how much I appreciated all she had done for me throughout my life. She lived another thirty years, so the thanks just kept piling up, and it made us both feel very good. Don't get me wrong. There were many things about my mother that bothered me over the years, but I kept focusing on the good things. When she died, I felt an enormous sense of peace. I had given her validation. I had told her how much she meant to me. Nothing was left unsaid when it came to my love for her.

I know many of you may feel, "Why would I thank my parents? They're horrible!" Keep in mind that you are in this world only because they brought you into it, and, even if only for that, they deserve your thanks. Parents do the very best they can, given who they are as human beings. This is not to

---

*I now realize that it wasn't too late. I often feel his presence, and I tell him over and over again how much I love him and appreciate all he contributed to my life. This gives me peace.

excuse inconsiderate, abusive, or neglectful parents, but if we keep in mind that parents go through life with their own fears, insecurities, and pain that may cause their horrible behavior, perhaps we will feel some compassion for them. Compassion makes it so much easier to say thank you.

So I suggest that you make a list of all the people in this world who have contributed to your life in some way, and thank them. If you "die before [you] wake," as the above prayer suggests, or if they die before they wake, you will feel a peaceful sense of having contributed to their lives in a very meaningful way.

If you are having a difficult relationship with someone in your life, you would be wise to heal it. If he or she has no interest in healing it, you can do it on your own, long distance, by closing your eyes and frequently sending radiant light his or her way emblazoned with the thought, "I love you." Even if you don't feel any love for this person, just the repeating of the words "I love you," over and over again, helps heal the hurt you feel. It may take a number of times before the anger completely dissolves, but if you do it often enough, the anger disappears as the love takes over. Whether this person can take in such an energy of love or not is irrelevant. You have sent your love and in that gesture lies your own peace of mind.

I can't give you a scientific explanation as to why the repetition of the words "I love you" can make such a difference, but I do know that doing so is powerfully healing. Perhaps it is simply changing the negative energy within your being into a positive energy. The words "I love you" move us from the anger of the Lower Self into the realm of the Higher Self, where beauty is always found. In my own life, when I feel anger toward anyone, I simply close my eyes and imagine him or her standing right before me. As I keep repeating to myself the words "I love you" I can feel the anger melting and my heart opening. Beautiful!

There are definitely times when we can't heal the body . . . either our own body or that of someone we love. But nothing can stop us from engaging the Spirit and healing the heart. From that place, we can find joy in the midst of any suffering that life can hand us.

Well, that's all I want to say about death. It wasn't that bad, was it? In fact, I hope I have even given you a laugh or two, as well as some courage to actually "embrace that hearse" with the realization that death can be a loving and peaceful experience, an extension of life, and a great opportunity for growth and healing.

There certainly is much more to be said about the process of dying and I suggest you investigate further. My intent here was to take away some of your resistance to exploring this important topic and thus help you gain a deeper understanding and certainly a deeper level of comfort. Once you have made death your friend, I believe you will have come a long way toward embracing your life and all the uncertainty it entails.

Life and death . . . how sweet they both can be!

enjoy the riches enjoy the riches enjoy the riches enjoy
the riches enjoy the riches enjoy the riches enjoy the
riches enjoy the riches enjoy the riches enjoy the riches
enjoy the riches enjoy the riches enjoy the riches enjoy
the riches enjoy the riches enjoy the riches enjoy the
riches enjoy the riches enjoy the riches enjoy enjoy the
riches enjoy the riches enjoy the riches enjoy the riches
enjoy the riches enjoy the riches enjoy the riches enjoy
the riches enjoy the riches enjoy the riches enjoy the
riches enjoy the riches enjoy the riches enjoy the riches
enjoy the riches enjoy the riches enjoy the riches enjoy
the riches enjoy the riches enjoy enjoy the riches enjoy
the riches enjoy the riches enjoy the riches enjoy the
riches enjoy the riches enjoy the riches enjoy the riches
enjoy the riches enjoy the riches enjoy the riches enjoy
the riches enjoy the riches enjoy the riches enjoy the
riches enjoy the riches enjoy the riches enjoy the riches
enjoy the riches enjoy enjoy the riches enjoy the riches
enjoy the riches enjoy the riches enjoy the riches enjoy
the riches enjoy the riches enjoy the riches enjoy the
riches enjoy the riches enjoy the riches enjoy the riches
enjoy the riches enjoy the riches enjoy the riches enjoy
the riches enjoy the riches enjoy the riches enjoy the
riches enjoy enjoy the riches enjoy the riches enjoy the
riches enjoy the riches enjoy the riches enjoy the riches
enjoy the riches enjoy the riches enjoy the riches enjoy
the riches enjoy the riches enjoy the riches enjoy the
riches enjoy the riches enjoy the riches enjoy the riches
enjoy the riches enjoy the riches enjoy the riches enjoy
enjoy the riches enjoy the riches enjoy the riches enjoy
the riches enjoy the riches enjoy the riches enjoy the

# 9

## Enjoying the Feast!

⚭

*Look. This is your world! You can't not look.*
*There is no other world. This is your world; it is*
*your feast. You inherited this, you inherited*
*these eyeballs; you inherited this world of color.*
*Look at the greatness of the whole thing. Look!*
*Don't hesitate—look! Open your eyes, don't*
*blink, and look, look—look further.*

CHOGYAM TRUNGPA[1]

There are certain quotes that not only touch our hearts, they also wake us up and make us take notice. Certainly, the above quotation is one of them. Most of us are asleep when it comes to the "greatness of the whole thing." You just have to look around to notice that we are given so much but we appreciate so little.

In *End the Struggle and Dance with Life,* I describe a number of ways in which we can learn to embrace all the blessings in our world. I urge you to study and use what I have written there. Of course, there is always so much more to be said about such an important subject and so many dif-

ferent ways in which we can increase our sense of appreciation. I want to devote the rest of this chapter to helping you
LOOK, LOOK, LOOK further . . . and preferably in the right
direction.

---

## THE "FOCUS ON THE RICHES" EXERCISE

Yes, life is uncertain but with absolute certainty I can tell you
that there are blessings to be found everywhere. The problem
is we are so habitually focused on the bad that there isn't
enough room in our brain to focus on the good! All you need
to do is change your focus from bad to good and the difference in your life will be dramatic. (Of course, this is what I
meant by "looking in the right direction"!)

Whenever my father tried to teach me something that I
didn't quite understand, he used to joke, "I'll draw you a picture." So in case you don't understand, here's a picture of
what your life will look like if you focus mostly on the BAD,
BLEAK, AND BLAH (B) with just a few moments of GOOD,
GREAT, AND GRAND (☺) interspersed . . .

LIFE

BBB☺BBBBBBBBBBBBBBBBBBBBBBBB☺BBBBB
☺BBBBBBBBBBBBBBBBBBBBBBBBBBBB☺BBBB
BBBB☺BBBBBBBBBBBBBBBBBB☺BBBBBBBBBBB
BBB☺BBBBBBBBBBBBBBBBBBBBBBBBB☺BBBBB
☺BBBBBBBBBBBBBBBBBBBBBBBBBBBB☺BBBB
BBBB☺BBBBBBBBBBBBBBBBBB☺BBBBBBBBBBB

Yes, a few good moments pop through, but, all in all, life looks pretty BAD, BLEAK, AND BLAH. Now let me draw you a picture of what it looks like as we reverse the process and begin focusing on the GOOD, GREAT, AND GRAND . . .

LIFE

☺☺☺☺B☺☺☺☺☺☺☺☺☺☺☺☺☺☺☺☺☺☺☺B☺
☺☺☺☺☺☺B☺☺☺☺☺☺☺☺☺☺☺☺☺☺☺☺☺B
☺☺☺B☺☺☺☺☺☺☺☺☺☺☺☺☺☺☺☺☺☺☺B☺
☺☺☺☺☺☺B☺☺☺B☺☺☺☺☺☺☺☺☺☺☺☺☺
☺☺B☺☺☺☺☺☺☺☺☺☺☺☺☺☺☺☺☺☺☺☺B
☺☺☺☺☺B☺☺☺☺☺☺☺☺☺☺☺☺☺☺☺B☺☺

A big difference, indeed! (You can tell I'm having fun writing this book!) Make no mistake about it . . .

Your experience of life reflects what you pay attention to.

If you're paying attention mostly to the BAD, BLEAK, AND BLAH, your experience of life reflects a life that doesn't seem to be worth living. If you're paying attention to mostly the GOOD, GREAT, AND GRAND, it reflects a wonderful life. And make no mistake, what you pay attention to is really up to you.

It seems to me that we must all make a conscious effort to focus on the good instead of the bad. This sometimes takes a great deal of creativity, as there is much in life that doesn't look as though it can offer us any good at all. But, as you have already learned, no matter how bad life gets, there is ALWAYS good to be found. Of course, what you may not realize and what is very significant is this . . .

NO MATTER HOW *GOOD* LIFE GETS, MOST OF US STILL ARE OBLIVIOUS TO THE BLESSINGS IN OUR WORLD.

And that's a waste of a beautiful life!

In the previous chapter, I suggested you create an "I HAVE HAD THIS" jar filled with experiences that helps you realize that life is NOT passing you by, so that you are better able to "embrace the hearse." You can see how this same exercise also helps us to "embrace the blessings." So no matter what is happening in your life, remember to . . .

BEGIN PAYING ATTENTION TO THE BLESSINGS.

And as you go through the day . . .

JOT DOWN THE BLESSINGS ON
LITTLE PIECES OF PAPER.

And at the end of the day,

ADD THESE LITTLE PIECES OF PAPER
TO YOUR "I HAVE HAD THIS" JAR.

What might these little blessings consist of?

good food
shelter
a sunny day
a rainy day
friends
work
television
books
flowers
cars
clothes
smiles
compliments
moments of sweet silence
acts of kindness to others
the telephone
nature
computers
hot water
life
cheese
candles
warm blankets
shoes
elevators
birthdays
art

music

toothpaste

massages

and on and on and on.

Soon you will need to increase the size of your "I HAVE HAD THIS" jar . . . which will give you much pleasure indeed!

Remember, you cannot have more or less than you take from the moment. I ask you, what are you going to take? Will your life look like BAD, BLEAK and BLAH (B) . . . or GOOD, GREAT, and GRAND (☺)? It depends *entirely* upon you.

---

### THE "BECOME A HEDONIST" EXERCISE

Unfortunately, hedonism has been given a bad rap. We can blame Aristotle who considered hedonic happiness "a vulgar ideal, making humans slavish followers of desires."[2] Boo, Aristotle! Perhaps he didn't have a *Webster's College Dictionary* that defines hedonism as "the doctrine that pleasure or happiness is the highest good." That's certainly a doctrine that has disappeared from the Western world! One could argue that hedonism doesn't stand alone as the highest good, but taking in pleasure surely belongs way up there as an important part of a life well lived.

And I speak of our ability to take the time to enjoy, value, appreciate, relish, and get pleasure from all the beauty around us. In today's world, this ability seems to be absent from our experience of life because, as I mentioned in the previous chapter, we don't take the time. In fact, I found a new word that seems to describe the psyche of our culture today. That word is "anhedonia." According to journalist Christopher Caldwell, the Greek root of this word means "without pleasure."[3]

It is a strange irony of modern society that the more we have, the less we seem to enjoy. Does that sound familiar? Overwork is part of this life-destroying syndrome.

When we overwork, by definition, we underenjoy.

That's not to say that our work cannot be enjoyable, but OVERwork deprives us of time for pure and simple, relaxed, unrushed fun and enjoyment and a more balanced life. As one sufferer reported, anhedonia "sucks the joy out of most things that make life worth living."[4]

When I worked with the poor in New York, I couldn't help but notice how appreciative of the smallest things so many of them were. It seems that the better our lives are in a material sense, the more we seem to take for granted. When we take things for granted, it is as though we are sitting at a banquet table and are starving because we can't see the food. I believe there truly is a point of diminishing returns. This means that, after a certain point, more and more and more money doesn't increase happiness. In fact, it can decrease it when we are consumed by work, work, work.

The reason for this is obvious. The more time we spend

on working to attain more, more, and more, the less time we have to enjoy, enjoy, enjoy . . . the less time we have to spend with friends, to curl up with a good book, to volunteer for our favorite charity, to enjoy nature and whatever other personal joys we are interested in. When we overwork, by definition, we lose a lot of the true joy in life.

So how do we change this bad habit of working too hard and bring more pleasure into our lives? As I see it, it is a matter of EXERCISING OUR WILL. By definition, those of us who are workaholics have no trouble whatsoever in exercising our will to work so hard. In fact, overwork has become a habit. Now we have to exercise our will to take time for fun and pleasure. As I just explained, this isn't easy to do, but it is essential that we do it. Isn't it strange that we have to work so hard to make time for enjoyment? Perhaps my friend Stewart Copeland was right when he said, "Work is easier than life!" Hmmmmm.

Here are a few examples from my own life that demonstrate that "We teach best what we want to learn most": As many of you already know, I tend to be a workaholic. In the middle of writing this chapter about the importance of kicking back and enjoying life, my friend, Donna, called to say that she and another friend were having coffee and I should come and join them. I told her no. I was in the middle of writing an important chapter. She asked what the chapter was about. I said it was basically about making sure we take the time to go have coffee with our friends! Needless to say, we laughed a lot but I didn't join her for coffee. (A perfect example of not "walking the talk"!)

Only an hour later, I looked at my calendar and noticed that in just two days time I was scheduled to meet with a good friend of mine, Jerry. We sometimes take time for a chat and a coffee from four to six in the afternoon at a magnificent sanctuary very close to my home. Again, my worry about finishing this book came forward, and I e-mailed him the following:

Dear Jerry,

Please forgive me, but I feel I must cancel our play date on Wednesday. I am under a lot of pressure to finish my book and need to focus. Give me a few weeks to feel a little more certain I will make my deadline. Trust me, I would much prefer playing with you!!!

Lots of love,

Susan

He had no idea that I was working on a chapter about the importance of making time for some "hedonic" pleasure, and here is his amazingly intuitive answer:

Dear Susan,

Okay. I understand. On the other hand, I really want to be a good friend who says trust ME, push you a little and remind you: this is your life (right now); it is important to take time off, especially a couple of hours at the end of the day. It will be good for you! (And me!) It will refresh you and make your work more productive. Okay, that said, I still understand if you need to cancel. Write me right back and say either (1) or (2) or (3).

(1) Okay, it will be good for me; see you at 4 P.M.

(2) Okay, but let's meet from five to six.

(3) I really must cancel for now.

Love from here.

Jer

Are you curious as to which choice I made? Pat me on the back. It was number 1! Let me hear some cheers out there. I am cheering myself. I realize that if my book is late, it's late. But if I don't spend time with my friends, I am losing the important balance needed for a life well lived.

Understand that this was a big step for me. It is easy for me to sit in front of my computer and work. It took *an exercise of my will* to break out of my work habit and put a little pure pleasure in my life. So you see, beautiful people out there, this isn't easy . . . even for me. It's ridiculous, isn't it? But that's how far the pendulum has swung on the side of work. We need to bring our lives back into the realm of appropriate once again, where life is full, rich, and balanced.

I understand that some of you can't walk away from your desks in the middle of the afternoon when you are not your own bosses. But there is still much one can do to keep focusing on the truly important things in life. A young woman once wrote to me and asked the following question . . .

My boyfriend and I both have such demanding jobs, we barely see each other these days. How can we reconnect again?

Even our relationships are compromised when the focus is too much on work. Here was my response . . .

This is a very common complaint in today's busy world. Couples have to become very, very creative in order to keep their love alive!

First, both of you need to ask yourselves: "Do I really have to work so hard or is it that I simply can't say 'NO' to extra tasks I am given?" If it is the latter, FEEL THE FEAR AND SAY NO ANYWAY! If your constant overworking is a requirement of the job, you may want to think about changing jobs.

Second, become a romantic. There are many ways to connect even when apart. For example, you can use e-mails to "loving" advantage. Every day . . . yes, every day . . . my husband and I send each other romantic e-mails expressing our love and thanks. My heart sings every time I receive one. Find creative ways to let your sweetheart know he is in your heart even when you are apart.

Third, save the weekends for each other. Obviously, we sometimes have to "catch up" with other things on the weekend, but so many couples go off in separate directions—even when they have the opportunity to be together. Every now and then, create special weekends just for the two of you. If you want to make a relationship work, it has to be a top priority in your life.

Fourth, when you are together, focus on the good stuff. Don't waste your time blaming, arguing, or lamenting. Focus on what's wonderful. Keep the romance high with candlelit baths, long walks, intimate talks, and lots of cuddling. Here's your goal: Make your time together so wonderful that, by hook or by crook, you will "magically" find ways to create more and more time to be together.

Again, this isn't easy to do when you are out of the habit of focusing on things other than work (and work includes being an at-home parent). But once we get a taste of pleasurable activity, we don't want to go back to the old way of being. We desire a more balanced way of being.

There are those who argue that what is truly important is not pleasure, but a sense of well-being that comes from a sense of meaning and purpose. Thankfully, this is not an either-or situation. I don't understand why people are so intent on either-or philosophies. In this case, we can have both . . . a time for great pleasure while also enjoying a great sense of meaning and purpose. They are BOTH important to a life well lived.

So here's the plan . . .

FIRST SCHEDULE TIME FOR PLEASURE. THEN *USE YOUR WILL* TO KEEP TO THIS IMPORTANT SCHEDULE. NO CANCELING ALLOWED!

Little by little, as we put balance in our lives, we will take the "AN" off of "ANHEDONIA" and find ourselves in a heavenly hedonic state of being in this world.

## THE "SAVORING" EXERCISE

Not only do we need to take the time for pleasure, we need to learn how to truly enjoy. Many of us have forgotten how. I was speaking recently to a woman who quit her demanding job and she was describing the difficulty she had de-stressing. She had forgotten how to enjoy. She said that it took her quite a while even to SEE beauty again. For example, when in an overwork mode, she used to go to the flower shop, rush in, get what she needed, and rush out. She said that now she isn't so rushed, she is finally getting to the point where she can actually SEE the colors, SMELL the smells, ENJOY the wonder of it all. Her experience has taught her the high cost of "success" in today's world, and she is determined never to let her joy be obliterated again.

So how do we increase our sense of pleasure when we have a bad case of "anhedonia"? Clearly we have to increase our ability to "savor." Here are two suggestions to get you started.

a) "Mmmmmmmm" is the sound of savoring. Conjure up in your mind that wonderful moment when you bite into something that tastes sublime and the sound of "mmmm-mmm" comes from your vocal cords. That is a wonderful example of savoring . . . truly *taking in* all the pleasure. We can expand our "savoring base" to cover all aspects of our life including a kiss from our partner, a beautiful sunset, a day off from work, and on and on and on. Most of us savor much too little and are hassled much too much. We have to turn this all around. I want to hear the sound of "mmmm-mmm" coming from everyone reading this book.

b) "WOW!" is a word for savoring. We think of it as a word heard mostly from children. That's a pity! Do they know how to savor more than we do? If so, we can learn from our children! So begin inserting the word "WOW!" into your vocabulary and also embracing the feeling of "WOW!"

WOW! Look at the sunset!
WOW! What a great meal!
WOW! What great friends I have!
WOW! I'm feeling better today!

You get the point. You don't have to wait for the big bursts of glory. Let the smallest joys invade your being. Remember this: We can make wealth a reality through appreciation.

I ask you, wouldn't it be wonderful to hear "mmmmm-mms" and "WOWS" circling the globe? I ask you to do your part in making this a reality.

WOW!

How great it all is!

## THE "LESS, LESS, LESS" EXERCISE

I was so impressed with comedian Jerry Seinfeld's response when he was asked in an interview if he was sorry about leaving his long-running, very successful television show. He said . . .

Why should I be sorry about something beautiful? There's a time to leave something and move on. Why do we always need more, more, more?

Good question. More, more, more is awesome when it comes to the enjoyment of the riches before us. But much of our unhappiness in life comes from our need for more, more, more in a material sense. Are we really that much happier driving expensive cars than more economical ones? Not when we are killing ourselves to pay for the expensive cars! If we are overworked, we definitely need to reverse our direction and go for less, less, less.

My husband, Mark, and I have recently decided that we wanted to need less and enjoy more. The word that is helping us greatly is the word, "ENOUGH." In an earlier chapter, I talked of the power of the word MAYBE; now we must add the word "ENOUGH" to our list of powerful words. So Mark and I are down-scaling in many ways. For example, we are emptying our closets of things we are not using and NOT replacing them with more things we won't use. We decided that instead of buying each other things for birthdays or other holidays, we will buy each other experiences. This means activities that we can do together to enhance our enjoyment of life and our relationship.

I have found that for all of us, despite our economic status, this need for more, more, more has become destructive in terms of our ability to enjoy life. So it would serve us all well to see if we can alter our course and fully enjoy what's on our table, literally and figuratively. I know that in an age of intense consumerism, it is hard for us all to curb our appetite for material things, but as we begin to work less and enjoy more, we understand the wisdom of the word "ENOUGH."

It is a strange phenomenon that our ability to need less increases our ability to enjoy more.

When we rush from thing to thing, when we work so hard to buy more, more, more, we are reducing our ability to appreciate anything in our lives.

So your task now is to begin, step by step, to create a less, less, less world for yourself so that you can be enjoying your life more, more, more.

---

### THE "SETTLING MIND" EXERCISE

---

The thinking mind is a very valuable thing. For many of our needs, it serves us well. But there are those times when it gets out of our control and tries to drive us crazy. We want to scream, "Shut up already! You're torturing me!" In the Hindu tradition, this undisciplined mind is likened to a drunken monkey. In *Feel the Fear and Do It Anyway*, I was kinder. I named this incessant voice, "the Chatterbox," and for good reason . . . it never stops chattering! It's enough to give you a headache.

If only the Chatterbox chattered about love and clarity and abundance and beauty. How grand that would be! Instead, it is constantly spewing out messages of doom and gloom and overload that do not allow us to think clearly and elegantly and joyously and flowingly. Most importantly, it doesn't allow us to create a GOOD, GREAT, and GRAND (☺) kind of world for ourselves.

When the Chatterbox is rattling on, one gets the feeling of a very cluttered brain. It's the kind of clutter that is very disorienting. Mess in our closets, on our desks, in our kitchens, is very disorienting at times, and mess in our minds is perhaps the biggest mess of all! An old Western philosopher summed it up nicely when he said . . .

I think, therefore I am Confused.[5]

How can we have a sense of appreciation when the incessant chatter in our mind makes us feel vulnerable, unsure of ourselves, and very confused? Our decision-making is muddled and, worst of all, we are not experiencing joy in our lives. That is because there isn't enough room in our heads to take in the magnitude of the abundance all around us. And if we don't take in the abundance of the now, we become more and more frightened that life is passing us by . . . and it is!

To help us embrace all the uncertainty in our lives, we have to learn how to stop this negative form of hyperactive behavior and enter into a mind-set of stillness, peace, and clarity. By now, I'm sure you have learned that this is not so easy to do. In fact, it is so hard to do, that entering such a mind-set is the basis of at least three Eastern philosophies . . . Confucianism, Buddhism, and Taoism.[6] Actually a lot of my thinking and inspiration comes from these philosophies, and I suggest you delve into them as well.

As I said earlier, many of the tools I have discussed in prior books are very effective in helping to clear the clutter of the mind. Let me now give you one more exercise that will help you empty your mind and allow you to be fully present in the now.

I "invented" this exercise while on a beautiful walk near my home in Southern California. There was wonder all around me, but I couldn't take any of it in. My head was a swirl of clutter, which included thoughts of contracts, deadlines, decisions to be made, and on and on and on. Thankfully, I became conscious of how overloaded my head was. It felt as though there was clutter totally filling my brain, preventing me from seeing, hearing, or doing anything with clarity. I was taking a beautiful walk, but my head was not enjoying or taking in a moment of it.

Finally, I asked myself, "What would happen if I could get rid of all the clutter swirling around my head? What if I could let it all simply float down like swirling snowflakes? Would that help?" So, as I walked, I imagined the swirling clutter as "snow" settling down until my head was totally clear . . . totally empty. I imagined myself having an empty glass head. Relief, indeed! But there was more than just relief.

All of a sudden, I became part of the glorious scene around me . . . the expanse of ocean, the magnificent weather, the color of the flowers, the striking cloud formations, the smell of eucalyptus, the palm trees "waving to me" in the breeze, the people running, walking, skateboarding, biking, enjoying the day. Instead of feeling removed from the scene, as one does with clutter in the mind, I became a part of it all. In fact the scene was moving *through* my empty head . . . I wasn't simply looking at it. The beauty was almost more than I could take and tears of gratitude welled up in my eyes. What had I done to create this miracle of vision? It was very easy. I simply made room for my head to take in what was happening around me.

The image that came to mind after this experience was one of those "snow domes," the little glass balls that you can shake up until they are filled with flakes that look like snow. When you stop shaking the dome, little by little, the specks float to the bottom until the glass ball is clear. Let me draw you another picture (My dad would be proud!) . . .

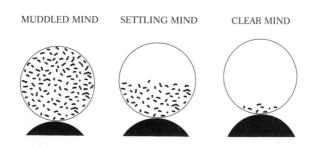

MUDDLED MIND     SETTLING MIND     CLEAR MIND

As you can see, there is little room in a Muddled Mind to take in anything. The Settling Mind is making room for new sights, ideas, and emotions to come through. The Clear Mind is ready to embrace the now.

So try this little exercise the next time your mind is taking you away from the present. As you become conscious of the Chatterbox trying to drive you crazy, just imagine your head as a glass ball filled with flecks of "thoughts." Then imagine these flecks slowly settling down until you are of Clear Mind. Here are a few examples:

You are watching a good movie, but your mind is cluttered with thoughts of all you have to do for a party you are giving next week. Let the thoughts float down and actually SEE the movie! You might truly enjoy it!

You are taking a beautiful warm bath, but your mind is on the problems one of your kids is having at school. Let the thoughts float down and let in the awareness of the warm water soothing your body, the scent of the beautiful bath salts you have sprinkled in the water, and just focus on the blessed moment of peace. You will deal with your child's problems better in a peaceful state of mind.

You are at a dinner party and are feeling very self-conscious about the impression you are giving to everyone around you. You are worried about how you look, your table manners, and what you are saying.

Let these self-absorbed thoughts drift down and down and down until your mind is cleared. You will then be able actually to hear what others are saying, you will be able to appreciate the effort made by your host or hostess to provide a beautiful party, you will be able to "give" your time and attention to those around you, and you will actually be able to participate and enjoy yourself.

These examples show how you can actually transform your experiences as you clear your head and allow yourself to be more vibrantly present. I am reminded of that very popular story about a Spiritual seeker who went to a Zen master wanting to learn about Zen. The master invited the seeker to tea. The seeker went in with a mind full of thoughts, ideas, and preconceived notions which he eagerly began to spew out to the master. Soon the master began to pour the tea, and he continued pouring until the cup was overflowing. The seeker noticed what was happening and yelled, "Stop! The cup is already full!" The Zen master pointed out to the seeker that his mind was like the overflowing teacup. How could he take anything in when his mind was alread y full? Point well taken!

As I said earlier, we need reminders to use the tools that can so effectively help us to transform our lives. So you may want to buy yourself one of those little glass balls to remind you how easy it is to clear your head. (Yes, we really do need all the reminders we can get!) Shake it up often to remind yourself how clutter blocks your vision and how clarity opens it up so that you can actually get into this world in a wonderful way.

## THE "LAUGHING BUDDHA" EXERCISE

As many of you already know, I am a lover of the Laughing Buddha. The more somber representations of the Buddha don't touch me in the same way that the Laughing Buddha does. As it is, we all take life much too seriously! Because of my love of the Laughing Buddha, I've placed a number of them around the house as a reminder to lighten up and enjoy it all.

I have a wooden Laughing Buddha on my night table next to a picture of my laughing husband (who is also a Laughing Buddha), a gorgeous pink quartz Laughing Buddha on my desk, a magnificent amber Laughing Buddha on my husband's desk, and a very large stone Laughing Buddha sitting in the courtyard outside my kitchen window. The one thing they all have in common is that they have learned how to "enjoy the feast" and they have no worry about the future.

My outdoor Laughing Buddha is the one that never ceases to amaze me. He is laughing when the rain pours down on him. He is laughing when the sun bakes down. He is laughing when we put a Santa hat on him at Christmastime. There is nothing that takes away his laughter. I know he would be laughing even if a tree fell on him and crushed him into a million pieces. I would be crying, but he would be laughing! Obviously, the Laughing Buddha has learned that "it's all happening perfectly"! The spirit that emanates from his smile is one of trust, appreciation, and inner joy.

I believe the Laughing Buddha represents the inner intelligence that lives within us all. He represents the part of us that is in tune with the Grand Design. He doesn't try to control the chaos. Instead, he listens and moves comfortably within the chaos as the world unfolds around him. He stays open to a constant flow of "joyous survival" versus "turbulent survival." He makes us realize that we can't get rid of the chaos, but we can get very creative with the turmoil. We are all the creators of how we want to see this world.

As still another reminder, I suggest you purchase a Laughing Buddha. They come in all sizes. A little one to put on your desk or next to your bed would suffice. Understand that the Laughing Buddha is not a religious symbol, as Buddhism is not considered a religion by many people who enjoy and benefit from its teachings. It can be seen as a philosophy or a way of seeing the world. For many, Buddhism is one way of becoming more enlightened about life. There are Jews, Catholics, Protestants, and others who embrace the teachings of Buddhism.

Once you acquire your Laughing Buddha, make sure you pick it up every time something is troubling you and ask yourself what the Laughing Buddha would tell you. I know you will find an answer that will lift you out of your upset and elevate you to a more cosmic space. That's what the Laughing Buddha does for me.

To take it one step further, you can pretend you are the

Laughing Buddha. My husband, Mark, was having difficulty with a few people in one of his projects, and he decided that instead of letting it get him down, he would go to work as the Laughing Buddha. To him, that meant radiating a happy, loving energy no matter what was happening in the office. He created a list of his favorite "happy" affirmations. Every day, he would repeat them over and over again. He would also e-mail me a message from himself as the Laughing Buddha.

The little game he was playing became our private joke, but the effect on his experience at work was very healing. He was actually able to deflect the negativity of the people in his project and embrace the happy nature of the Laughing Buddha. This enabled him to interact with everyone in a much more positive way. His demeanor changed so much that his assistant jokingly asked him what drugs he was taking! Mark just smiled.

We can all play the Laughing Buddha game in any area of our lives. Each time we play it, it shows us how to stay in the Highest part of who we are for longer and longer periods of time. Powerful stuff, so rewarding, and a lot of fun.

It is clear that appreciation of today is one of the most powerful tools for helping us embrace tomorrow. So take it all in. And once you do, you will be astounded by what you have been missing in this life, right here, right now. I keep going back to the telling words of Emily Dickinson . . .

As if I asked a common alms
And in my wandering hand . . .

A stranger pressed a kingdom
And I bewildered stand.

These beautiful words tell us that when we finally open
our eyes, we stand bewildered by the riches in front of us.
Life is beautiful . . . open your eyes to it all.

it's all about love it's all about love it's all about
love it's all about love it's all about love it's all
about love it's all about love it's all about love it's
all about love it's all about love it's all about love
it's all about love it's all about love it's all about
love it's all about love it's all about love it's all
about love it's all about love it's all about love it's
all about love it's all about love it's all about love
it's all about love it's all about love it's all about
love it's all about love it's all about love it's all
about love it's all about love it's all about love it's
all about love it's all about love it's all about love
it's all about love it's all about love it's all about
love it's all about love it's all about love it's all
about love it's all about love it's all about love it's
all about love it's all about love it's all about love
love it's all about love it's all about love it's all
about love it's all about love it's all about love it's
all about love it's all about love it's all about love
it's all about love it's all about love it's all about
love it's all about love it's all about love it's all
about love it's all about love it's all about love it's
all about love it's all about love it's all about love
it's all about love it's all about love it's all about
love it's all about love it's all about love it's all
about love it's all about love it's all about love it's
all about love it's all about love it's all about love
it's all about love it's all about love it's all about
love it's all about love it's all about love it's all
about love it's all about love it's all about love it's
all about love it's all about love it's all about love
it's all about love it's all about love it's all about
love it's all about love it's all about love it's all
about love it's all about love it's all about love

# 10

## Let God Worry About It!

∞

*Good morning, this is God. I will be handling*
*your problems today. I do not need*
*your help. Have a good day.*

—GOD[1]

I suspect that even if we received the above message
directly from the Source in all of His or Her glory, we
would still feel compelled to step in and take control, control
freaks that we are. Oh, wouldn't it be wonderful to have the
trust that God in His heaven is handling our problems today
and every day of our lives?

What about you? Do you believe in God? If you are like
so many students who have attended my various seminars
about overcoming fear, you would answer this question with
an emphatic "Yes!" My next question would then be, "If you
truly believe in God, then why are you afraid?" And, again, if
you are like so many of my students, there would be a look of
confusion on your face.

Perhaps a more telling question would have been, "Do you trust God?" I don't think there would have been as many emphatic yesses in the room! The truth is that although the American dollar bill says, "In God We Trust," there are few Americans, or, for that matter, few people in the Western world, who truly put their trust in God. *Belief* and *trust* are two very different things.

Of course, you may be someone who simply has no belief or trust in God whatsoever. There are many people who don't. This is neither good nor bad. However, I can't help but feel that it would take a lot of weight off your shoulders to believe in and trust something "bigger" than yourself. I don't know anyone who wouldn't like some "higher help" while walking through this fascinating and often difficult maze called life. And between you and me, if we look around, how can we deny the existence of *something* out there . . . a Higher Power, a Universal force, Universal Light, or Universal Intelligence . . . that creates the miracle of this world and the miracle of life itself? The thirteenth-century philosopher Rumi observed that . . .

> When we talk about God, we're like a school of fish, discussing the possible existence of the sea.[2]

There is just too much that nourishes and supports us to deny the existence of *something* . . . whatever that something is. Trust in a Higher Power is not a necessary ingredient for a beautiful life, but it is very valuable in helping us embrace all the uncertainty we face throughout our lives.

Before I suggest some ways in which you can enhance

your ability to "let God worry about it," let me get up on my soapbox and say a few words about organized religion. You may or may not agree with what I have to say, but I feel it will help explain why so many have pulled away from organized religion generally in recent years.

Certainly one reason for their pulling away is the perception that God is noticeably absent in their houses of worship. Too many religious leaders feel that there is only one way to be in the presence of God . . . and that is THEIR WAY. And it is in this kind of thinking that prejudice, judgment, anger, and exclusion are born, the perfect ingredients for alienation and hostile acts. *A loving God would strongly disapprove!*

It was in the 1600s that the philosopher and mathematician Blaise Pascal said . . .

Men never do evil so completely and cheerfully as when they do it from religious conviction.

Chilling, but true. And nothing much has changed over the years. We don't have to look very far in order to see how religious dogma is behind so much of the misery in the world today. I suspect that if ALL houses of worship were to become more tolerant, loving, accepting, inviting, caring, and respectful of others who believe differently, many who have left their own houses of worship would eagerly return.

There is the story of a priest who ran a parish in Manhattan. He was dismayed by the empty seats in his church. He put an ad in the *New York Times* inviting Christians who felt wounded by the Christian church to come on a Tuesday night to talk about it. He hoped at least thirty would show up.

Instead, 450 showed up![3] I suspect that the more love that emanates from any religion, the more popular it will be.

And then there is the Bible. The Bible was written by human beings who obviously had prejudices of their own. It is filled with stories which, *in their proper context*, may help readers learn some valuable lessons. Unfortunately, some take these stories literally. And that can be very dangerous.

To illustrate, I received a very humorous, yet telling, "open letter" posted by an unknown source on the Internet. It concerned the conflict between radio personality Dr. Laura Schlessinger and the gay community. Schlessinger, who is described as "an observant Orthodox Jew," agrees with many in the Orthodox Christian community, that homosexuality is an abomination according to the Bible (Leviticus 18:22) and should not be approved of under any circumstances. The following are a few excerpts from that open letter responding to Schlessinger's observation about homosexuality and the Bible.

Dear Dr. Laura:

Thank you for doing so much to educate people regarding God's Law. I have learned a great deal from your radio show, and I try to share that knowledge with as many people as I can. When someone tries to defend the homosexual lifestyle, for example, I simply remind them that Leviticus 18:22 clearly states it to be an abomination. End of debate.

I do need some advice from you, however, regarding some of the specific Bible laws and how to follow them.

I would like to sell my daughter into slavery, as sanctioned in Exodus 21:7. In this day and age, what do you think would be a fair price for her? She's 18 and starting University. Will the slave buyer continue to pay for her education by law?

I know that I am allowed no contact with a woman while she is in her period of menstrual uncleanliness (Lev. 15:19–24). The problem is, how do I tell? I have tried asking, but most women take offense.

Lev. 21:20 states that I may not approach the altar of God if I have a defect in my sight. I have to admit that I wear reading glasses. Does my vision have to be 20/20, or is there some wiggle room here? Would contact lenses help?

Most of my male friends get their hair trimmed, including the hair around their temples, even though this is expressly forbidden by Lev. 19:27. How should they die?

The author of this letter goes on to provide a number of additional examples and ends with . . .

I know you have studied these things extensively, so I am confident you can help. Thank you again for reminding us that God's word is eternal and unchanging.

So much for taking the Bible literally! I hope you are laughing, not throwing tomatoes at me. I think the above is a very humorous way of pointing out how dangerous it is for humankind to assign the word of God to a book written by human beings so many years ago.

"But, Susan, I love my religion, and I love the Bible!" Let me make it clear that I don't want to discourage or insult any of you who make religion an important part of your life. Religion and the Bible have helped so many through so much. If you derive joy and love and meaning and solace, and, most importantly, a sense of trust from it all, that is wonderful. Hang on to it. It is serving you well.

Keep in mind that you could also serve your religion well by being a force for positive change. For example, if you hear your religious leaders speaking unlovingly about the beliefs of others, make your feelings known. I believe that when religious leaders are forced by their parishioners to stop behaving in an unloving, hence unGodly way, people will eagerly flock back to their houses of worship. As I see it . . .

If it isn't about love, it isn't about God.

I know some of you may be thinking, "Susan, how do YOU know if God is loving or not?" Good question. I clearly don't know . . . and neither does anyone else! However, when I think of God in a loving, nourishing way, I find much solace and strength, as will you. Again, I quote Hugh Prather, who so wisely said, "Why be right instead of happy when there is no way to be right!"[4] Certainly when we think about God, there is no way to be right, but there is a way to be happy.

Now that I've stood on my soapbox about religion and the Bible, let's look at what this chapter is really about . . . *embracing a Higher Power that we can trust and that can help us face all the uncertainty in our lives.* Even if you have absolutely no belief in God in the traditional sense, I would like to present various ways of trusting in some form of a Higher Power in the hope that it may ease your worry about all the uncertainty in the world and give you comfort.

## THE "TAP INTO THE LIGHT" EXERCISE

You may be wondering what my personal concept of a Higher Power is. A little background: I am Jewish by birth and pulled away from my religion in my teens because of the prejudice and righteousness I saw in those who had an "our way is the right way" kind of attitude. Of course, I noticed that this prejudice encompassed not only those who practiced my religion but all other religions as well. As I pulled away, I became free to embrace what is most loving in all religions and philosophies and let the rest go. While this may or may not be right for others, it has worked beautifully for me.

Even though I am not a religious person, I have a strong belief in a Higher Power. I experience it as a healing radiant Light that surrounds the entire Universe. This Universal Light is always there for me (and everyone else) to tap into. I find that when I tap into this Light, I draw into myself the most positive energy one can imagine. In this powerful energy, I know there is nothing to fear. Obviously, it serves me well to remember to tap into the Universal Light on a constant basis!

How did I come to this way of experiencing a Higher Power? When I was young I pictured God as a man in white robes with a long white beard who was there to answer my prayers. I must say he was terribly inconsistent. Sometimes he answered my prayers and sometimes he didn't! Given his inconsistency, I was woefully confused about it all. And as I grew into adulthood, I was unsure whether I believed in God or not. But then one day something happened that convinced me that God was absolutely there for me, but not in the "form" I had previously imagined.

I had, sadly, just separated from my first husband and decided to take a vacation in Spain to clear my head. Having been very dependent on my husband, I was filled with great trepidation about traveling without him, but I felt the fear and did it anyway. (This was long before I wrote the book!) As I stood alone one morning in the garden of the Alhambra looking at the beauty around me, I was suddenly bathed in an overwhelming radiant Light that seemed to have come from nowhere. I felt myself blissfully dissolving into the oneness of the Universe and into a sublime sense of peace and safety. It was as if the Light had embraced me and told me without any words being spoken that I had nothing to fear.

This mystical experience lasted only a few moments, but I knew I had touched a new dimension of my being, a part of me that was able to connect with a Higher Power . . . and my Spiritual Journey had begun. No longer did I envision God as a man in white robes with a long white beard who was there to answer my prayers. From that moment on, I saw God as a powerful, healing Light that is there *whenever I remember to tap into it*. This means that whenever I find myself bogged down in Lower Self thinking, I only have to close my eyes and imagine the Light all around and within me. I am immediately transported to a Higher Self frame of mind, and all is well. Heaven!

Out of curiosity, I asked a dear friend over lunch how she "sees" God. She answered that she sees God in the form of a benevolent father who watches over us and fills the world with beauty. She says that her confusion lies in the horrors of the world. How could God allow such horror to exist?

Obviously, she is not alone in her confusion. Many have great difficulty in believing in God because of all the horrors in the world. I recently saw a satirical article which explained that God MUST have "bipolar disorder"![5] Bipolar disorder is a severe psychological problem characterized by cycles of depression that are awful for the sufferer and his loved ones and cycles of elation that are wonderful for the sufferer and his loved ones. What else could it be?

I told my friend about this article and we both had a good laugh. I then told her my concept . . . that it's not a matter of God coming down and guiding us; rather, it's about our reaching up and pulling into our being the peace and power and love and learning that are always there for the taking.

Let me share with you one way I have devised for myself to tap into the Light. The only thing you need for this exercise is the great power of your imagination.

First close your eyes.

Then, in your mind's eye, imagine a magnificent all-encompassing Light, with the radiance of the sun, that envelops the entire Earth. Imagine it to be a Universal Light of healing, health, love, joy, and all good things.

Then, take a deep breath and instead of exhaling through your mouth or nose, exhale by pushing your breath through a large imaginary hole at the top of your head. Visualize your breath shooting upward and connecting with the radiance of the Universal Light.

Then visualize yourself inhaling this magnificent

Light, again through the top of your head. Feel the Light filling your entire body and radiating outward through your pores touching the world around you.

Keep repeating this process until you feel a sense of peace and strength and love.

My friend tried this exercise and loved it. I suggest that you try it as well. I suspect you, too, will love the feeling of the radiant Light of the Universe flowing throughout your being. It is a feeling that gives you the confidence that you can handle whatever life hands you. And it is very reassuring that this radiant Light is yours for the taking. Most of us walk around with a cloud over our head. It's time now to walk around with a radiant glow around and within us. It makes all the difference in the world.

## THE "SEND THE LIGHT" EXERCISE

As we bring the Light of a Higher Power into and around ourselves, we can also send this healing Light to others. I do this all the time. I send Light to those who are ill or hurting in any way. I send Light to strangers who seem to be having problems in life. I send Light to those I love. I send Light to those who have made me angry (and soon I'm not angry anymore). When I send Light to others, I feel a sense of closeness and connection. Can you imagine a whole world of people sending love and Light to one another? Beautiful.

How do you send the Light to others? Simply alter the above exercise as follows:

Close your eyes.

Then, in your mind's eye, imagine a magnificent all-encompassing Light, with the radiance of the sun, that envelops the entire Earth. Imagine it to be a Universal Light of healing, health, love, joy, and all good things.

Then, take a deep breath and instead of exhaling through your mouth or nose, exhale by pushing your breath through a large imaginary hole at the top of your head. Visualize your breath shooting upward and connecting with the radiance of the Universal Light

Then visualize yourself inhaling this magnificent Light, again through the top of your head. Feel the Light filling your entire body and radiating outward through your breath and through your pores all the way to the person of your choice.

In your mind's eye, see the Light encompassing the both of you, creating a feeling of healing, love, and caring.

Bathe in this wondrous Light together and watch the love grow and any walls that are there come tumbling down.

Sometimes you may stand apart, sometimes you may hug, sometimes you may cry. In any case, a wonderful feeling of connection is established.

I have found this practice of sending radiant Light to others a very healing thing to do. I don't know if it's healing to them, but it certainly is to me! I believe you will find it healing as well. So whether you believe in this form of a Higher Power or not, I urge you to try sending Light to others.

Ultimately you can do this exercise with your eyes wide open. You will find yourself sending Light when entering a roomful of a strangers, when enjoying a family dinner, when walking down the street, when in an interview . . . everywhere! I find it incredibly useful to send this warming Light to my audience as I begin a workshop. I immediately feel connected. This blissful connection certainly feels better than when my knees used to knock and fear enveloped my entire being! So try sending this wonderful healing Light to those around you. It is an awesome form of connection.

## THE "TURN IT OVER" EXERCISE

This is an exercise that helps us to build trust in a Higher Power. As I said earlier, believing is not enough. Learning to trust is the essential ingredient. That's where we usually fall short.

If we try to control everything on our own (which, of course, we can't), we get very weary and very discouraged and very frightened. Once we can feel comfortable turning our worries over to a Higher Power in whatever form that feels right for us, we feel the weight of our world being lifted from our shoulders. In effect, we say to ourselves, "Take over, God. I trust it's all happening perfectly." This is our acknowledgment that we can't see the bigger picture, the Grand Design, and we really don't have any control over so many outcomes in our life. This kind of "surrender" is a tremendous relief.

The way I have used this exercise is as follows: When I find myself worrying about something in my life, such as money, a speaking engagement, one of my children, flying in a plane, or world events, I am quick to realize that I am forgetting to turn my problems over to a Higher Power. When I realize the problem . . .

> I close my eyes.
> Then cut an imaginary cord that is attaching me to whatever I am worrying about.
> I then say to myself, "Okay, God, I am doing my best. I'll let you take over now."
> I take a deep breath and feel myself letting go (this step is very important).

As I turn my problem over in this way, I feel an immediate sense of relief.

Certainly the key here is to *remember* to turn it over, which is why I have always stressed repetition of the exercises I present to you. Our ultimate goal is to remember this exercise very early in the worrying game so that the minute a worry enters our mind, we can immediately cut the cord to the worry and "let God worry about it."

One of the pitfalls is that so many of us are able to turn it over, but then we take it back, and the worry begins anew. We, then, have to again remind ourselves, for as many times as it takes, that it's time to let God worry about it instead of allowing it to drive us crazy.

Another pitfall is that we selectively trust. "Oh, I'll trust God with this, but not that. I'll trust God with my finding a husband (or wife), but I won't trust God with my money . . . no way!" This is one arena where we have to learn how *to go all the way* in order to find the peace we are looking for.

So we need to keep practicing and practicing and practicing until turning it over becomes an automatic action. Even then, we never stop the practicing. There's always the part of us, the Lower Self, that wants to take control.

The Lower Self doesn't trust anyone or anything, including itself, which is why it worries so much. It is in the Higher Self that our ability to trust lies. And when the Higher Self meets a Higher Power . . . WOW! It is then that we are in touch with the incredible strength that we have to handle all that life hands us. There is no greater security than that.

It serves us all to make the decision every morning "to turn it over" before we even open our eyes . . . before we start feeling torn apart by the difficulties that life is handing us. When we are able to turn it over, we make lots of room in our minds to think in a way that is courageous, loving, satisfying, and joyous. Not a bad way to go through the day!

---

## THE "PERFECT PRAYER" EXERCISE

---

Prayer is a valuable way of helping us to embrace uncertainty. So I strongly suggest that you give prayer a try. The healing effects of prayer, *even for those who do not believe in God,* have been documented in a number of scientific studies.[6] So even if you don't believe in God, pray to the Spirit or Higher Self within or simply to the Grand Mystery of it all, but don't negate the potential power of prayer in your life.

Perhaps you have been disappointed by prayer in the past. If so, it is almost a guarantee that your prayers were of the "petitionary" type . . . that is they asked for something to be a certain way . . . *your way, not God's way.* Sometimes petitionary prayers are answered; but often they are not. For example, when I was young, I prayed that my parents would live forever. Well, they didn't live forever. Obviously, this is a prayer that could never be answered. Yes, they are alive in Spirit and in my memories, but I wanted them to always be *physically* present so I could give them a big hug and a kiss. It doesn't work that way.

We have to learn to pray not with a sense of wishing, hoping, yearning, or entitlement, but with a sense of trust, gratitude, and purpose. If you don't know such a prayer, you're in luck! *In End the Struggle and Dance with Life,* I presented such a prayer which I will repeat for you now." ("Thank you, Susan.") It is a prayer that will never let you down. Slowly, read it aloud right now, and feel the words enter your being . . .

> "Dear God. I trust that no matter what happens in my life, it is for my highest good. And no matter what happens in the lives of those I love, it is for their highest good. From all things you put before us, we shall become stronger and more loving people. I am grateful for all the beauty and opportunity you put into my life. And in all that I do, I shall seek to be a channel for your love."

How could you ever be disappointed with a prayer like that? No expectations, only a sense of trust and gratitude and purpose. If we began and ended every day with this prayer, and "lived it" throughout the day, the quality of our lives would improve dramatically.

I suggest you keep a copy of this prayer in your wallet, beside your bed, on your desk, and wherever you feel it will be noticed. Just keep repeating it over and over again until you memorize it. It is a prayer that will bring you peace.

## THE "LOVE CONNECTION" EXERCISE

If you truly want to FEEL a sense of God, whether you believe in God or not, take notice of how you FEEL when you act in loving ways. It is a feeling like none other. Sublime. It is a feeling of connection and happiness in its purest form. Symbolically, it is truly embracing the Light of a Higher Power and letting it flow through you to embrace others.

Let me tell you about an interesting experience I had the other day that illustrates this beautifully. Impulsively, I did something very loving for a needy stranger. She looked at me in shock and surprise, and exclaimed, "Are you an angel? I just know that God sent you to me." I answered, "No, I'm not an angel, but maybe God did send me to you. After all, how come I showed up just when you needed me?" And I thought to myself, *Why did I show up at just the right time? Coincidence? Maybe. Maybe not! Who knows?* But I certainly feel that when we act in loving ways, the Light of a Higher Power is working through us. And it does feel sublime. So even if you don't believe in God in the traditional sense, perhaps you could embrace the concept of God as Love coming through us. To me, concepts of God and Love are interchangeable.

There is no question that all the bells and hoops and ceremonies and rituals, the robes and statues, and incense and gongs, found in our houses of worship create a very appealing atmosphere. And the tradition of going to our church or temple or mosque once a week or more can be a great reminder as to what it's all about (and we certainly need reminders!). It is important, however, in the middle of all the fanfare, that we don't lose sight of WHY we are sitting in a house of worship to begin with . . . and *that is to help keep us on the path of Love.*

Obviously, one does not need a house of worship to be able to stay on the path of Love. So whether you belong to an organized religion or not, you need to ask yourself the following question as you go through each day . . .

### How can I be more loving here?

And, of course, follow up with appropriate action. As you fill your consciousness with loving thoughts and you act in loving ways, you are allowing the Love of God, the Force, the Light, or whatever it is for you to flow through you. As you experience this flow of Love, you will discover a sense of peace and fulfillment unlike anything you have experienced before.

Let me end this chapter by saying that all of the above are ideas and suggestions based on my own experiences. There is no right or wrong way to believe in God. We all have to experience a Higher Power (or not) in a way that is most comfortable and reassuring to us. If it is in the form of an old man with a white beard and flowing robes, that's fine. If it is in the form of a woman sending loving energy throughout the world, that's fine. If it is in the form of Universal Energy, Universal Light, the Grand Design, the Force, or whatever, that's fine.

But whether you believe in a Higher Power or not, I suggest you just look with wonder at the Great Mystery of it all, and, with thanks, stand in awe.

JOY AHEAD! JOY AHEAD! JOY AHEAD!
JOY AHEAD! JOY AHEAD! JOY AHEAD!
JOY AHEAD! JOY AHEAD! JOY AHEAD!
JOY AHEAD! JOY AHEAD! JOY AHEAD!
JOY AHEAD! JOY AHEAD! JOY AHEAD!
JOY AHEAD! JOY AHEAD! JOY AHEAD!
JOY AHEAD! JOY AHEAD! JOY AHEAD!
JOY AHEAD! JOY AHEAD! JOY AHEAD!
JOY AHEAD! JOY AHEAD! **JOY AHEAD!**
JOY AHEAD! JOY AHEAD! JOY AHEAD!
JOY AHEAD! JOY AHEAD! JOY AHEAD!
JOY AHEAD! JOY AHEAD! JOY AHEAD!
**JOY AHEAD!** JOY AHEAD! JOY AHEAD!
JOY AHEAD! JOY AHEAD! JOY AHEAD!
JOY AHEAD! JOY AHEAD! JOY AHEAD!
JOY AHEAD! JOY AHEAD! JOY AHEAD!
JOY AHEAD! JOY AHEAD! JOY AHEAD!
JOY AHEAD! JOY AHEAD! JOY AHEAD!
JOY AHEAD! JOY AHEAD! JOY AHEAD!
JOY AHEAD! **JOY AHEAD!** JOY AHEAD!
JOY AHEAD! JOY AHEAD! JOY AHEAD!
JOY AHEAD! JOY AHEAD! JOY AHEAD!
JOY AHEAD! JOY AHEAD! JOY AHEAD!
JOY AHEAD! JOY AHEAD! JOY AHEAD!
JOY AHEAD! JOY AHEAD! JOY AHEAD!
JOY AHEAD! JOY AHEAD! **JOY AHEAD!**

## 11

# Making It a Good News World

∞

*Give us a happy ending and we write*

*a new disaster story.*

BARRY GLASSNER[1]

We live in a bad news world. No doubt about it. Everywhere we turn we are constantly assaulted with news of impending danger, whether it's . . .

- contaminated food

- road rage

- recession

- deadly diseases

- homicidal strangers

- sadistic cops

- sadistic criminals

- acts of terrorism

- kids that kill

- impure water

- cars that kill

- a weak military

- the end of the world

- and on and on and on.

I'm sure you could add a few of your own "favorites" to the list. No wonder we have trouble embracing uncertainty . . . there only seems to be danger ahead!

Of course, all of the above need to be appropriately addressed, but I suggest that . . .

The threats of our demise are greatly overexaggerated and/or erroneously reported!

As you have already learned . . . maybe I'm right or maybe I'm wrong. Only time will tell for sure. But in the meantime, I refuse to give up my power to find the good news that is always there in unbelievably large measure. While we are wise to take certain protective measures relative to what is happening in our world, we are also wise to understand that it is all a guessing game. And why not "guess" good news instead of bad news?

And who are the bearers of all this bad news? The media, the politicians, the advertising industry, advocacy groups, and everyone else who realizes that *the more frightened we are, the more it makes us want to support their cause, their popularity, and/or their bank account.* For example, I recently received an advertisement for a how-to book about health. On the cover of the brochure was emblazoned the words, "READ THIS OR DIE." I didn't read it and I didn't die!

Perhaps this was an incredibly valuable brochure, but why the outrageous scare tactics? A few days later, I received an advertisement for a book on finances. It said, "READ THIS OR GO BROKE!" (Both publishers must use the same advertising agency.) My habit when I get such fear-motivated messages is immediately to throw them in the garbage where they belong. Why? Because my "gut" tells me that such negative energy can't be good for me!

In my opinion, the news on television is one step away from being the worst offender. As Barry Glassner points out, the producers of local newscasts live by the rule "if it bleeds, it leads."[2] There is a desperate need for creating drama out of the drab that hopefully will keep us watching. Reporters on the evening news go from one nightmare story to the next and we can now get twenty-four hours a day of disaster on our twenty-four-hour news channels. We should congratulate ourselves that we have the courage to walk out the door!

But let's move on to what I consider the absolutely worst offender of all. The winner in the Worst Offender Department goes to . . . THE BAD NEWS IN OUR MIND! Like the producers of local news shows, our minds also live by the rule "if it bleeds, it leads." While you can turn off the bad news on television with the remote control, there is no such device to turn off the bad news within our own heads. Our minds chatter on endlessly as we tell ourselves all sorts of disaster stories about our lives not working. Obviously we haven't taken the advice of some very wise person who said . . .

> If you want to see if your life is working, place a mirror under your nose and if it fogs up, it's working.

I like this approach. It makes life much simpler. Too many of us take a much more complicated approach as we convince ourselves that life is filled with doom and gloom. We focus only on the bad and pay no attention to the good. It goes without saying (but I'm saying it anyway), that the bad news in our minds cheats us out of so much of the joy in living.

I'm curious: Just where did all the good news go . . . both in the media and in our minds? Trust me, the good news is there, it's all around us. *It's just that the bad news seems to get all the attention.* It's time now to put the bad news in the background and the good news in the foreground. We can start by telling ourselves an important truth, which is . . .

> We in Western society live amazingly wonderful lives!

Really, we do! Let me just skim the surface . . .

- Most of us eat very well—too well, if our obsession with dieting is any indication!

- We live much longer than human beings have ever lived before.

- We can effectively control so many diseases with the miracles of modern and alternative medicine.

- Most of us live in a free society.

- Our world has expanded incredibly through the miracles of technology.

- More than ever before, people are traveling far and wide to explore this big, wide, beautiful world.

- Flowers bloom, mountains soar, and skies give us a changing masterpiece every day of the year.

- Millions and millions of people perform intensely beautiful, generous, loving, and caring acts every day of the year.

- And what is most encouraging . . . the world is filled with wondrous possibility and the ever-present opportunity to change what is Bad News to what is Good News.

Again, I'm sure you could add a few of your own favorites to the list. Can you see that in so many ways . . . ALL IS WELL? Yet if we paid attention only to the bad news in the media and the bad news in our minds, we would think that we had died and gone to Hell. Who wouldn't be in a state of paralyzing fright? The fact is . . . there is so much good news around us that it would stagger the imagination, that is, IF WE PAID ATTENTION!

While it's true that we can't control the bad news fed to us by so many sources in the outside world, we can certainly control the bad news we allow into our psyche. That is, we can learn how to lessen our focus on all that is, or could be, bad and magnify our focus on all that is, or could be, good. If you think about it logically, this should be a very easy thing to do. After all, why would one want to focus on the bad when focusing on the good *feels* so much better?

Few would really want to, but as you may have already discovered, creating a Good News World in your mind isn't as easy as one would think it should be. It actually requires an intense training period. Our minds seem to be addicted to bad news, and you know how difficult it is to overcome addictions. *Our assignment now is to become addicted to good news.* Since we won't find much help in the outside world, it's up to us to help ourselves.

Let me give you an added incentive to make this assignment a top priority in your life. We are increasingly looking for ways to keep our bodies healthy. And the evidence is piling up that . . .

Good news in the mind creates good news in our bodies; conversely, bad news in the mind creates bad news in our bodies.

Dr. Renata Mihalic has been a great teacher of mine in this area of body-mind connection.[3] Dr. Mihalic is formally trained as a chiropractor, but she doesn't do the "cricking and cracking" of the neck and spine that many chiropractors do. Her healing hands masterfully and gently relax the tense muscles that often cause problems in the neck and spine . . . and everywhere else. And more often than not, it is the bad news in our minds that creates the tense muscles to begin with. As the muscles relax, the pain disappears, the body's energy begins to flow, the immune system is bolstered, and soon, "ALL IS WELL"—body, mind, and Soul.[4]

Most of us assume that negative thinking affects only our mental health, which is important enough; after all, it does rob us of our enjoyment of life. What we don't fully realize is how much our negative thinking also affects our *physical health*. We don't fully understand that the bad news in our heads can create our stiff necks, stomachaches, headaches, and, over time, much worse. Our muscles tense, our stomachs churn, and our immune system is compromised with the "emergencies" created by the thoughts in our head.

It is understandable that the body reacts physically to physical stress. For example, when you begin to fall, an "antifalling" response kicks in. This response is perfect for the protection of your body. Adrenaline surges, your arms reach out automatically to protect yourself from harm, and all the other protective reflexes come into play. Once you gain your balance, the stress disappears, and your body shifts into business as usual.[5] This is normal. This is healthy.

Dr. Mihalic has taught me that what we must also understand is that the body also reacts *physically* to *mental* stress. Let's assume your mind is troubled about an argument you just had with your partner. A similar "antifalling" response is activated, causing physical stress. You kiss and make up, at which point you regain your emotional balance, the stress disappears, and your body shifts into business as usual. Again, this is normal. This is healthy.

But now let's assume that the mind continues to be troubled about many factors in your relationship. You live with the mental and physical stress all day long and you go to sleep with it at night, that is, your "antifalling" response keeps . . .

working and working and working and working and working and working and working and working and working and working and working and working and working and working and working and working.

Are you exhausted yet? You get the picture. If you keep this emotional stress up long enough, the body gets very tired and eventually your physical health will be compromised.

This miracle body of ours is well equipped to handle the short bouts of stress—both physical and mental—that we regularly experience. So there is no need to concern yourself about the short periods of "bad news" we handle every day of our lives. Good and bad are simply part of life. It's the long bouts of bad news that we need to address.

I was speaking recently with a woman whose husband left her ten years ago. Yes, divorce is difficult. It requires a short period of "mourning," of dealing with many stressful issues, and then it's time to move on—body, mind, and Soul. This woman had obviously never moved on, and the quality of her life—and her body—has suffered greatly. Ten years, and no end in sight, is a long time to stress the body with anger, pain, and sadness. She obviously never learned the valuable lesson that we all need to learn . . .

Happiness is the best revenge!

It is also the best medicine for the body.

If you observe the body of someone who has just received some wonderful news, it's an uplifting sight. His or her energy is dancing, radiating with joy. The body is clearly affected in a positive way. If you look at the body of someone who has just received some bad news, it's a very different picture. You can actually see a physically "down" response. The body constricts and speech can be muddled and slow. There is no joy here. The body is clearly affected in a negative way.

Again, while we can't control the world around us, we can certainly learn how to respond to all things—yes, ALL THINGS—in a health-affirming way. We have the power to create a life that feels good, rather than one that feels bad— despite the actual circumstances in our lives and in our world. Temporary times of stress are normal. But as we survey the situation and find the gifts that are inherent in all things, the stress disappears. When we learn how to find the gift in all things, by definition, we are happier, more excited about life, more open to change, and eager to embrace the future. I hope I have convinced you of the value of creating a Good News World. If not, read the above again and again and again.

There is a Universal law that tells us "Like attracts like." With this in mind, do we really want to walk around giving and getting the negative energy of a Bad News World? I don't think so. The energy field is something I have talked about in all my books because it is such an important factor in becoming a powerful and loving human being. And, as you have just learned, it is such an important factor in maintaining a healthy body.

I created the following exercises along with all the other exercises in this book to help you create the Good News Habit. I know that some of these exercises may seem too simple (or silly!) to be effective, but try them and you will see how powerful they truly are. The biggest challenge is to remember to do them! And again, how quickly we forget!

## THE "PROTECTIVE FILTER" EXERCISE

a) For a while in my own personal growth, I drastically lowered the amount of negative news that I watched on television or read in newspapers and magazines. And that was perfect for my own progression into becoming a more positive person.

Then at some point I was able to create simple protective "tricks" that allowed me to keep my eyes wide open to the bad news in the world without it destroying my peace of mind. This was important to me, as I love to feel as though I am a part of the world . . . and it's hard to feel a part of the world when you don't have a clue as to what is going on! One of the tricks I created was the Protective Filter exercise which combines the miracle of glass plus the miracle of imagination. This simple exercise allows me to be a part of it all without being upset by it all. Let me explain.

Glass is an amazing product. Think about windows. Whether in our home or car, they protect us from noise, cold, wind, sleet, snow, rain, and all the negative elements. The amazing things about windows is that, not only do they enrich our lives by protecting us from the "bad news" outside, they enrich our lives by inviting in the "good news"—the light, the sun, and the view. I told you this was a miracle product!

Another miracle "product" is the imagination. If used properly, it allows us to conjure up all sorts of ways of shielding ourselves from the bad news and letting in the good. Of course, if used improperly, it does the reverse. But we are truly in control of our imagination and we need to learn how to use it in a way that supports rather than sabotages us.

In this exercise, I combined the miracles of glass and imagination in a way that allows me to watch the news in a "protective" fashion. I first imagine a glass shield between myself and the television set. Then, as the bad news drones on and on, I imagine this glass shield stopping the negativity but at the same time allowing the salient information to come through. It also allows the few items of good news to come through as well. Think about it: With a little help from an imaginary piece of glass conjured up by my mind, I can be open to, yet protected from, all the bad news that is around me.

I suspect you are thinking, "Susan, you've been working too hard!" I suggest you try it out. In fact, use the imaginary piece of glass to protect you not only from the negativity of the television news, but from the negativity in all situations in your life . . . during a family spat, driving in your car, talking on the phone, reading the newspapers, walking down the street, and so on.

b) Here's a variation. If the image of the glass shield doesn't work for you or if you want an alternative, you might like the image of a protective bubble of light. I often use this as well. Close your eyes for a moment and in your mind's eye see if you can create a beautiful bubble of light around your entire body. Beautiful, isn't it? Wherever it is called for, imagine this wonderful shield of light around you, protecting you from the bad and letting in only the good.

If you don't like either image, let your imagination find the perfect protective image that is right for you. The point is that . . . *you are in control of what you let into your energy field.* And as Dr. Mihalic points out to me all the time . . .

If you take care of your field, your field will take care of you.

This Protective Filter exercise is just one way of taking care of your energy field.

## THE "PERPETUAL STUDENT" EXERCISE

The concept of the "observer" or "witness" is an important one to understand. Yes, when we become observers, we take ourselves one step away from the drama. And as you read in earlier chapters, becoming observers also allows us to let go of expectations and to create a sense of wonder instead of fear about the future. There is something else that becoming observers allows us to do, and that is to become perpetual students—always learning and always growing.

Here's an example of how it all works: Let's imagine that we are bombarded with news of a potential environmental crisis. Instead of becoming caught up in the drama, we can see ourselves as students studying the why's and wherefore's of the environment. We may also investigate what we can do to help, such as how we can change our lifestyle to improve the situation.

So instead of, "Help! I pray it won't affect ME!," it becomes, "Hmmm. I wonder how this will all turn out and if there is anything I can do to help." You can see the difference relative to stress on our bodies. (Yes! The wonder of wondering!)

> The first is a closing, a tensing of the muscles as a feeling of helplessness kicks in. The second is an opening, a willingness to learn and grow . . . and a willingness to participate in the solution.

This is healthy for our own lives and for the environment as well. If we see it all as education and participation, our minds can operate in a much more constructive fashion. Education and participation . . . not fear and frustration.

So become a student of the world around you. In this way life becomes exciting, challenging, and filled with meaning and purpose. What an exhilarating way to go through life!

---

THE "SPREAD GOOD NEWS" EXERCISE

One of the ways in which we can create a healthy, supportive, and expansive energy field is to be the one who actually is the "spreader" of good news. In this way, you can never get away from it . . . the good news, that is. The following are a few suggestions as to how you can do this in your everyday life:

a) *Affirm your intent to spread the good news.* Here are some affirmations that work beautifully . . .

I radiate light and love wherever I go.

I see the good in all things.

My actions put healing energy into the world.

If you repeat these affirmations over and over again . . .

1) They will become imprinted in your mind;
2) They will replace any negative thoughts you may have;
3) They will improve your self-confidence;
4) They will remind you to be the bearer of all beautiful news;
5) They will help you to create a positive energy that will touch everyone you meet along the way.

This is a stunning result from just repeating some beautiful words over and over again. As I have mentioned before, I find affirmations very powerful in terms of changing what doesn't work in my life.

b) *Thank others who "spread good news."* This includes those who spread good news as waiters, doctors, street cleaners, politicians, friends . . . anyone who has helped you in any way or provides a wonderful example of a loving and caring person. Phone. Write. Let them know how special they are. If it is appropriate, let their bosses know how special they are. People are so used to getting complaints; a compliment is a blessing, indeed. Spreading your thanks into the world is certainly a wonderful way of spreading good news.

---

## THE "JOY AHEAD" EXERCISE

There is no question that the world gives you the message, DANGER AHEAD. I'll bet you've never seen the message JOY AHEAD. So it's up to us to create that scenario for ourselves. We should put a sign everywhere we can see it . . .

### JOY AHEAD!

We read about DANGER on our child's soccer fields, DANGER in the food we eat, DANGER in nature, DANGER when we fly . . . DANGER. DANGER. DANGER.

What about JOY on our children's soccer field, JOY in eating the delicious food around us, JOY in nature, JOY when we fly? What a difference in terms of how we experience life!

I suggest you substitute the word JOY for DANGER wherever you can. Of course, there are times when it is essential to heed the DANGER AHEAD sign that tells us there is a problem on the road ahead, but we should be filled with JOY that someone put the sign there to warn us! See, you can make good news out of anything.

When we carry a DANGER AHEAD sign in our heads it is really a form of self-sabotage. The reality is that most of what we worry about never even happens. And even if "bad" things actually do happen, and, of course, they sometimes do, these so-called bad things can be handled in a life-affirming "good news" way. I'm sure you can think of many people who have experienced great difficulty, even tragedy, and with their uplifting attitude, they were able to turn the bad news into good news. They have learned that no matter what happens, we can create a JOY AHEAD world for ourselves . . . and that's REALLY good news!.

## THE "WHAT-IF-IT'S-GOOD" EXERCISE

This is really an extension of the JOY AHEAD concept. So much of our fear is created by the negativity of our "what-if" mentality as we contemplate the future. It's not that asking "what-if" is a bad thing. The problem is that our "what-ifs" never seem to be good! The following are typical "what-ifs":

> What if I lose my job?
> What if I get sick?
> What if I get a divorce?
> What if the weather is terrible?
> What if we have a lousy time?
> What if the food is bad?

You never hear in contemplating the future . . .

> What if I love my job?
> What if I'm healthy?

What if my marriage is loving?
What if it's a gorgeous day?
What if we have a fabulous time?
What if the food is great?

Of course it is wise to plan ahead so that we are not caught by surprise in terms of the curves that life sometimes throws us, but we can do this in a life-affirming, self-empowering way. And we can always imagine the best, knowing we can handle whatever happens . . . good or bad. So if you are a "what-if" kind of person, make your what-if's ring with wonderful possibility. Get rid of the pessimism, which is simply negative clutter in a mind that should be ringing with joy. Our bodies truly love a joyous mind!

---

## THE "DIFFUSE THE BAD NEWS" EXERCISE

---

We can learn how to lessen the stress on our bodies by diffusing the bad news within and around us. Diffusion looks like this:

"Yes, this is bad but there is some good we can find in all of this."

And then we set about finding the good. This lightens the load of negativity when friends, family members, and co-workers see things in a negative way. For example, if someone at your restaurant table complains about the lousy food, point them in a more positive direction by saying, "You're right, the food isn't that great. But aren't we lucky to all be together . . . and nobody has to clean up afterward!"

Immediately, the bad news is re-directed into a more positive place. And almost certainly you will feel the negative energy of the table rapidly become more positive. (I should warn you that some of your friends may hate your positive energy; they may prefer doom and gloom. If that is so, it's time to find new friends.)

In this way, we accept the bad and diffuse the negativity by somehow, some way, using it as a force for good. This is a frivolous example. We have to be very creative in more serious and profound situations, but the same principle applies. For example, we can take something as horrible as a war and create ways of healing the hates that created the war to begin with. Remember that . . .

So much that is good can come from so much that is bad.

Why the bad has to be there in the first place, I haven't a clue. But, given that it *is* there, happily we can find a way to diffuse the negativity by sprinkling it with the possibility that one day the good will overpower the bad.

It is important that we don't run away from the fact that bad things happen to all of us in one form or another. When we are in denial, the pain doesn't go away; it just festers within our bodies. When we bring the pain to the surface, our body rejoices. We enter the healing Land of Tears, and we feel release. You can see how holding up a huge wall of denial would be very detrimental to both the body and the mind. Exhausting! After we get in touch with the pain, we can then begin what I call life's treasure hunt . . . finding the good within the bad.

In a Bad News World, we are taught to avoid pain at all costs. We are taught that pain is dysfunctional. It isn't dysfunctional at all; it is a rich part of life that can ultimately bring us many good things. When we live in a Good News World, we know we will always get to the other side of the pain having gained a great deal of knowledge, confidence, strength, and peace.

---

## THE "MORE THE MERRIER" EXERCISE

I am a great believer in the group process. And I can't think of anything better than a Good News Group in terms of raising our spirits and keeping them raised. If you don't know of any to join, it's certainly easy to create one. Just pull together as few as three or four people, schedule a time and place to meet regularly, and create a few rules such as the following:

1) NO COMPLAINTS! Agree to talk only about the good things in your lives. Even if something difficult is happening, create a way of making something positive out of it.

2) Agree to make something good out of what is seemingly bad about events in the outside world . . . and talk about ways in which you can contribute to positive change.

3) Agree to thank each other. Support each other. Hug each other. Enjoy each other.

In this kind of positive energy, you meet to celebrate everyone's triumphs—big or small. You meet to enjoy the energy of friendships being created and goals being achieved. When you are around such energy, your own personal energy is fed and your good feelings soar.

There is no question that it is so much easier to embrace the uncertainty in your life when you are supported by a wonderful group of friends. Of course, there is value in other kinds of groups as well, but for the purpose of creating a Good News World for yourself, joining or creating a Good News Group will serve you beautifully.

## THE "SMILE A LOT" EXERCISE

The simple act of smiling is a superb aid as we build our Good News World. Think about it. How could you think bad news with a big smile on your face? Try it right now . . . put a big radiant smile on your face. I'll do it with you. There. Doesn't the world feel happier when you have a smile on your face? It certainly does for me. The French philosopher Alain painted a beautiful picture when he said . . .

> The smile reaches down as deeply as a yawn and relaxes one after the other, the throat, the lungs and the heart. A doctor would not be able to find anything in his medicine bag that takes effect so quickly, so harmoniously.[6]

Yes, not only does a smile make you happy, it's good for your health as well!

Of course, some of us forget to smile. I suggest that once again you pull out your pile of Post-its and write SMILE on a number of them, then place them on your mirror, your dashboard, your refrigerator, your desk, everywhere you can see them. When a smile becomes a much more regular fixture on your face, you can remove all the Post-its . . . but not until then.

SMILE!

It's a wonderful Welcome sign to a Good News World!

There is no question in my mind that creating a Good News World for ourselves is essential to our being able to embrace the vast amount of uncertainty we face in our lives. Creating a Good News World also allows us to have a lot more fun. You are now equipped with some entertaining tools to get you started. Enjoy!

it's yours for the taking it's yours for the taking it's
yours for the taking it's yours for the taking it's yours
for the taking it's yours for the taking it's yours for
the taking it's yours for the taking it's yours for the
taking it's yours for the taking it's yours for the taking
it's yours for the taking it's yours for the taking it's
yours for the taking it's yours for the taking it's yours
for the taking it's yours for the taking it's yours for
the taking it's yours for the taking it's yours for the
taking **it's yours for the taking** it's yours for the taking it's yours for the taking it's yours for the taking
it's yours for the taking it's yours for the taking it's
yours for the taking it's yours for the taking it's
yours for the taking it's yours for the taking it's yours
for the taking it's yours for the taking it's yours for
the taking it's yours for the taking it's yours for the
taking it's yours for the taking it's yours for the taking it's yours for the taking it's yours for the taking
it's yours for the taking **it's yours for the taking** it's
yours for the taking it's yours for the taking it's yours
for the taking it's yours for the taking it's yours for the
taking it's yours for the taking it's yours for the taking it's yours for the taking it's yours for the taking it's
yours for the taking it's yours for the taking it's yours
for the taking it's yours for the taking it's yours for the
taking it's yours for the taking it's yours for the taking it's yours for the taking it's yours for the taking
it's yours for the taking it's yours for the taking it's
yours for the taking it's yours for the taking it's yours
for the taking it's yours for the taking it's yours for
the taking it's yours for the taking **it's yours for the**

# 12

# Be Prepared!

∞

*If you knew that you could handle anything*

*that came your way, what would you*

*possibly have to fear?*

—SUSAN JEFFERS[1]

I find it fascinating that when I wrote my first book, *Feel the Fear and Do It Anyway*, I was told by the publisher to avoid the use of the word "Spirit" because it would put people off. And the publisher was probably right. Spirit wasn't "in" at the time. That left me with the task of putting what was basically a Spiritual message into words that didn't talk about Spirit! I managed to do it until I got to the last part of the book, where I couldn't resist and sneaked in a few words that spoke of the Spiritual part of who we are.

A number of years later when I wrote *End the Struggle and Dance with Life*, books that talked of the Spirit were wildly popular, and I didn't have to hide my Spiritual concepts any longer. I could include them at the beginning, in the middle, and at the end. You may be wondering what happened in those interim years that made Spirituality a concept so many people were eager to embrace. I believe we can attribute this shift, at least in part, to a growing collective yearning to connect with a place within where we could feel safe, complete, and fulfilled.

Most of us were unable to find that wonderful place within. We looked everywhere but couldn't find it. This is because society at large, including the schools that taught us and now teach our children, avoids the issue entirely as it focuses on competition and materialism. Religion, except for a few shining examples, also avoids the issue as it focuses on judgment and self-righteousness. Competition, materialism, judgment, self-righteousness . . . feelings all based on a fear mentality. They are hardly feelings of safety, completion, and fulfillment.

So where did many of us finally find what we were looking for? It wasn't sitting on a mountaintop, or in a church, or in a cave somewhere in India. Actually, it was in the bookstore, of all places. Here, in the rapidly growing self-help section, we began to find books that satisfied our deep yearning. And we gobbled those books up as if we were starving to death . . . and we were. The essential ingredient in many of these self-help books was a sense of the Spirit. Delicious! We had always heard about the threesome that defines us as human beings—Body, Mind, and Spirit. We already knew a lot about Body and Mind and now we finally found a way to learn about the Spiritual part of who we are. Completion, at last! As we began adding a Spiritual dimension to our Bodies and Minds, we slowly began to fill the hole in our hearts that we had painfully experienced before.

You might be wondering who writes all these Spiritually oriented self-help books. With few exceptions, the authors are ordinary people like me who have found some extraordinary ways of being in this world. Through various means, such as the study of Eastern philosophies, peak experiences, Spiritually led workshops, and/or our own personal triumphs and tragedies, we have all made some headway on this wonderful Journey inward and have an intense desire to pass on our amazing insights. We may vary in terms of our formal qualifications, our personal experiences, and the road we choose to get there, but what unites us all is that we are on the very same Journey toward that place of inner peace and inner power . . . the Spiritual part of who we are. And whether you realize it or not, you, too, are on the same Journey.

While some of us walk ahead and some of us walk behind, I am safe in saying that none of us are there one hundred percent. As I have said before . . . even the Buddhas have their days! We all have a great deal yet to learn. Each day brings us new challenges as to how we can better take responsibility for our experiences of life, which, I might add, is one of the ways in which we find this place of inner peace. As such it becomes an exciting Journey, despite the difficulties that life sometimes hands us.

"Self-help" is an apt description of the Spiritual path to power that we must all take to change what doesn't work in our lives. We need to celebrate the day we finally wake up and realize that, on Spiritual matters, no one can help us but ourselves. Self-help teachers can give us tools, but, by definition, *it is up to us to use the tools we are given.*

We must all learn how to "self-help ourselves" in order to find the best of who we are.

And it is well worth the effort.

I maintain that without a connection to the Spiritual part of who we are, there will always exist a deep emptiness that nothing in the outside world can fill. Without a connection to the Spiritual part of who we are, we will always feel a sense of dissatisfaction and yearning as we expect our husbands, our wives, our children, our job, food, money, or whatever to fill us up, but nothing does the trick. Also, without that connection, there exists a deep-seated fear of all that is happening or could happen in our lives, making it very difficult to embrace all the uncertainty in our world.

As I mentioned earlier in this book, the name I have given to the Spiritual part of who we are is the Higher Self. This is opposed to the Lower Self, the place of the ego, which hasn't risen above the clouds to see the beauty in life, nor is it able to see the power and love that lie within. It sees only the dark, the negative, and the scary. You can be sure that when we are feeling fearful, we are seeing with the eyes of the Lower Self. Our task then is simply to find our way to our Spiritual Home, the Higher Self.

I also mentioned earlier, that if I could take away one thing from everyone reading the book, it would be expectations, and if I could add one thing, it would be trust. As we become Spiritually grounded, (pardon the oxymoron) we learn, perhaps for the first time, just whom we can safely trust. And who is that? Since we have no control over the behavior of others, the answer is . . . no human being out there! Putting total trust in another human being is unwise and even unreasonable, as you may have already learned. So we must put our trust in ourselves.

Don't get me wrong. There are some people in our lives on whom we can count to "be there" for us most of the time. But for one reason or another, they may not be around when we need them most. Or they may have issues in their own lives that interfere with their being available to us. What we must under-stand totally, fully, and completely is that we can't trust anyone out there totally, one hundred percent, forever and ever.

I know you may not want to hear this. I certainly didn't! But when you realize how Spiritually powerful you are in terms of handling all that life offers you, there truly is no need to look elsewhere. Your place of safety lies within. This should give you a feeling of relief knowing that . . .

There is something inside of you—your Higher Self—that is always there to handle elegantly, beauti-fully, intelligently, powerfully, and lovingly, anything and everything that can ever happen to you.

Wow! Really emblazon this thought on your mind. And, as I mentioned earlier in this book, if we can see our Higher Self connected to a Higher Power, the sky is the limit when it comes to our living a magnificent life. It is this kind of think-ing that allows us to embrace all that has happened or will ever happen in our lives.

Now we know what we have to do. You've probably heard me say it before and I'll say it again: We must all learn the tools that open us to Higher Self thinking and then we need to use them. More than just "using" them, we need to make them an integral part of our being . . . a part of our thinking, acting, doing, seeing, hearing, and speaking. We need to incorporate them into every moment of our lives. Many of us start by practicing for twenty minutes in the morning or evening. And that's a good start. But our ultimate goal is to incorporate these empowering ways of being into every minute of every day. Again, most of us never get there one hundred percent, but it is clear to me that the more we learn how to think in a Higher Self way, the more joyous our lives will be. It's really that simple. It's a matter of tipping the scale, giving more weight to the best of who we are instead of the worst of who we are.

What brings us closer and closer to our goal is repetition, repetition, repetition. And that repetition needs to go on for the rest of our lives. The world is filled with negativity and we constantly have to strengthen our "Spiritual immune system" to keep it from becoming overwhelmed with doubt. And our Lower Self, which inserts itself into our minds every once in a while has to be stilled. We welcome it, calm it down, and then shower it with thoughts of power and love until it disappears, at least for a little while. It won't be long until it rears its scared little head once again, but with our Spiritual toolbox, we are always prepared.

I never feel bad when I repeat any of the valuable insights in my different books, tapes, or talks. And now you know why. It is because this information has to be heard over and over and over again. Even I need to hear it over and over again! Do you remember the wonderful story passed on by Marilyn Furguson?

A professor describes his teaching a new concept to his class. "I told them once, they didn't understand. I told them twice, they didn't understand. I told them three times . . . *and I understood.*"[2]

Yes, the statement "We teach best what we want to learn most" is certainly true when it comes to Higher Self principles. When I started teaching I "knew," but I hadn't yet understood. That is, I didn't experience the concepts deep within my being and I kept getting tripped up by my Lower Self thinking. As I taught and taught and taught, little by little I got an "Aha! Now I understand!" Of course, as I just explained, I don't as yet understand it ALL nor do I always act in a Higher Self way. (Trust me on that one.) That is why my loved ones tease me when I am lamenting a problem by saying, "Go read your books!" And they are right. More repetition is necessary even on my part to embrace the concepts I already know to be true. There is so much more to learn . . . for all of us. And we will continue to learn for the rest of our lives. If you think about it, that's part of what makes life such an exciting adventure.

The tools that I present here have only one purpose, and that is to transport you to the Higher Self. When you do any of the exercises in this book (or in any of my other books), you are shifting yourself into Higher Self thinking . . . you are finding your way Home. Your task is to accumulate and put into use as many Higher Self exercises as you can so that when life seems difficult, all you have to do is reach inside your "toolbox" and pick the tool that is most appropriate to what is happening at the time. No matter how difficult life may seem to be at any particular time in your life, there are ways of seeing that difficulty in a positive, life-affirming way. The eyes of the Higher Self see the possibility of beauty in all things.

So you can understand that the only kind of security that we can ultimately ever have comes from within. The only kind of freedom that we can ultimately ever have comes from within. Neither has anything to do with what is happening in the outside world. In fact, things may seem really lousy on the outside, but with the help of our Higher Self, we can make our world shine like a brilliant gem as we bring meaning and purpose to it all. Rising above any situation that the future may bring us is the height of security and freedom. And we all have the ability to do that.

The following are two exercises that set the stage for Higher Self living.

## THE "BE PREPARED" EXERCISE

Now that you better understand the principle of Spirituality and the importance of having Spiritual tools at your disposal as difficulties confront you in everyday life, your task is to fill your toolbox with powerful tools so that you are always ready to deal with what life hands you. The motto of the Boy Scouts is "Be Prepared." That's also a great motto for Higher Self living!

By the time you finish this book you will have forty-two exercises (tools) to put into your toolbox. This is IN ADDITION to the many, many tools I provide in *Feel the Fear and Do It Anyway, Feel the Fear . . . and Beyond*, and *End the Struggle and Dance with Life*. You are rich with resources! Each of the tools is meant to do the very same thing . . . to transport you to the Higher Self so that all things in your life can be handled in a life-affirming way. It looks like this:

HIGHER SELF

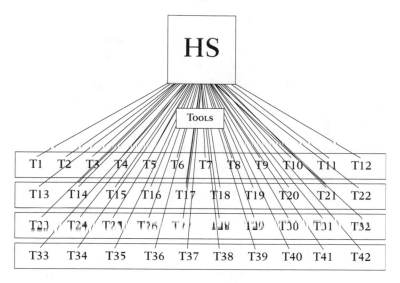

What do you do with all these tools? You certainly do not try to learn to use them all at once . . . that would really drive you crazy! Just begin with one or two of the exercises. Play with them, see if they fit who you are as a human being, and if they do, put them into your toolbox. I don't mean only your metaphorical toolbox. I know it may sound silly, but if I were you I would use an actual little box where the tools can be held. Simply write down the exercises that work for you on little pieces of paper and put them into your toolbox. Yes, you've heard me say it time and time again . . . how quickly we forget!

That Lower Self is firmly entrenched and we go there automatically. Sometimes it takes some comical antics to help us remember that we have a better way of being in this world. So keep adding to your toolbox—the real one and the metaphorical one. Each morning, look into it and emblazon on your mind all the means you have to go through the day in a powerful and loving way . . . despite what happens.

Your toolbox is a treasure chest. And the treasures inside are to be used over and over again, not stored away for years at a time until the Chatterbox in our minds make us desperate once again to take some action. If you begin to use the tools in your toolbox regularly, the "crisis" aspects of life will all but disappear. Yes, you may get moments of upset, but then you are able to quickly switch into a more nourishing way of thinking. And the word "nourishing" is a good one. These exercises are meant to feed us—Body, Mind, and Soul.

So start by picking a few tools that you are drawn to and begin practicing them until they become an automatic part of how your mind operates in this world. Then collect some more. Remember that there isn't only one way. What might seem right for one person may definitely not be right for another. It's a matter of trial and error. The "right" way is different for all of us. As time goes by, it is wonderful to collect a whole bunch of tools that will help you meet any of life's emergencies with a feeling of calm and wonder.

As you keep using these tools, change happens . . . or, as my friend, Robert Holden, says, "Shift happens"![3] (We have to keep our sense of humor.) Remember, all these exercises are meant to get you to the same place . . . to the best of who you are, your Higher Self. There are so many pathways to peace of mind. There are so many pathways to power and love.

The following exercise demonstrates how we put all the tools in our toolbox to use.

## THE "IT'S ALL PRACTICE" EXERCISE

All of life is your Spiritual classroom filled with opportunities for Spiritual practice. With all that is happening in your life you ask . . .

> How can I see this situation in a life-affirming way?
> How can I grow into a more loving and powerful person?

Everything that comes into your world is your opportunity to practice the tools you are learning . . . an optimal opportunity for "self-help." Yes, it's all Spiritual practice.

| PROBLEMS AND JOYS | OPPORTUNITY FOR: |
|---|---|
| You are having problems with your family. | > *Spiritual practice* |
| You have to get another job. | > *Spiritual practice* |
| You are planning your wedding. | > *Spiritual practice* |
| You are watching a beautiful sunset. | > *Spiritual practice* |
| You are worried about money. | > *Spiritual practice* |
| You are worried about all the violence in the world. | > *Spiritual practice* |

When you see life as a Spiritual practice, all news, *particularly bad news*, gives you the opportunity to explore the unused parts of yourself . . . new dimensions of being. Your mantra becomes . . .

Whatever happens, I will discover a new and wonderful part of myself.

Ram Dass gives us a wonderful example of how this works. A number of years ago, he chose to play a major part in the care of his dying father. In order to do this, he had to give up his plans for participating in certain Spiritual studies that he had been looking forward to with eager anticipation. But he said that instead of being an obstacle to his Spiritual practice, the care of his father WAS his Spiritual practice. He explored ways to honor his father, to keep his heart open, to handle the differences in their personalities, and to see it all as a gift. All lessons. And he used all the tools that were available to him to keep him on the path of learning and growing at those times when his Lower Self tried to take over and try to make him feel sorry for himself.

The Journey to the Higher Self is a very exciting one . . . and a very necessary one . . . if we are to live peacefully in a world filled with great mystery and uncertainty. When we approach all things with a Spiritual mindset, all is well no matter what is happening in our lives. In the beginning, don't expect to feel it in your bones. Again, the exercises will only penetrate the deepest part of who you are with constant use. Remember that we have to break a very bad habit . . . the habit of living in the lowest part of who we are.

It is fascinating that we live as two different people:

*As a Lower Self person,* we are scared.
*As a Higher Self person,* we feel as though we can handle anything that comes our way.

*As a Lower Self person,* we feel scarcity.
*As a Higher Self person,* we feel abundance.

*As a Lower Self person,* we feel empty.
*As a Higher Self person,* we feel fulfilled.

You get the picture. When things are not going as expected, your first step is not to try to fix it, but to access the Higher Self, THEN take action to fix it. First things first! This is how we learn that the outside world can do whatever it does, but we have the power to control our relationship to it all.

The big question is, "Will you make the commitment to make these exercises a part of who you are and how you live in this world?" That is a question only you can answer. I can give you some powerful tools as can other self-help authors out there, but it is your responsibility to use them.

One thing I can promise is that as you take responsibility for making your life one of Spiritual enrichment, your experience of life gets better and better and better. Again, I haven't met anyone who lives in the Higher Self ALL the time, but as we keep practicing and practicing, we live in this magical place more and more and more of the time.

So begin filling your toolbox now and continue to practice using the tools every day of your life. If you want to get rid of fear, loneliness, and a sense of separation and find your way Home, you have to have a deep commitment and intention to totally change the way you think about the world around you. This, of course, is easier said than done. It takes commitment and courage. And if I discover an easier way to get to the best of who you are, I'll let you know. And I'll trust you'll do the same for me!

**you can handle it all** you can handle it all you can
handle it all you can handle it all you can handle it
all you can handle it all you can handle it all you
can handle it all you can handle it all you can
handle it all you can handle it all **you can handle it**
**all** you can handle it all you can handle it all you
can handle it all you can handle it all you can
handle it all you can handle it all you can handle it
all you can handle it all you can handle it all you
can handle it all you can handle it all you can
handle it all you can handle it all you can handle it
all **you can handle it all** you can handle it all you
can handle it all you can handle it all you can
handle it all you can handle it all you can handle it
all you can handle it all you can handle it all you
can handle it all you can handle it all you can
handle it all you can handle it all you can handle it
all you can handle it all you can handle it all you
can handle it all you can handle it all you can
handle it all you can handle it all you can handle it
all you can handle it all **you can handle it all** you
can handle it all you can handle it all you can
handle it all you can handle it all you can handle it
all you can handle it all you can handle it all you
can handle it all you can handle it all you can
handle it all you can handle it all you can handle it
all you can handle it all you can handle it all you
can handle it all you can handle it all you can
handle it all you can handle it all you can handle it
all you can handle it all **you can handle it all** you
can handle it all you can handle it all you can

you can handle it all you can handle it all you can handle it all you can handle it all you can handle it all you can handle it all you can handle it all you can handle it all you can handle it all you can handle it all you can handle it all you can handle it all you can handle it all you can handle it all you can handle it all you can handle it all you can handle it all you can handle it all you can handle it all you can handle it all you can handle it all you can handle it all you can handle it all you can handle it all you can handle it all you can handle it all you can handle it all you can handle it all you can handle it all you can handle it all you can handle it all you can handle it all you can handle it all you can handle it all you can handle it all you can handle it all you can handle it all you can handle it all you can handle it all you can handle it all you can handle it all you can handle it all you can handle it all you can handle it all you can handle it all you can handle it all you can handle it all you can handle it all you can handle it all you can handle it all you can handle it all you can handle it all you can handle it all you can handle it all you can handle it all you can handle it all you can handle it all you can handle it all you can handle it all you can handle it all you can handle it all you can handle it all you can handle it all you can handle it all you can

# Epilogue:
# Bring It All On!

∞

*We went to heaven the long way round.*

—HENRY DAVID THOREAU

It's always difficult for me to end a book. For many, many months, my mind is totally focused on what I want to say to you. And when I type the last word into my computer, it's as though I am saying good-bye to my global family . . . at least until the next time. I don't have any *grand finale*, but I do want to share a few more thoughts before *I REALLY* say good-bye.

You have learned that the biggest supports for embracing the uncertainty in your life include wonder, curiosity, letting go, humor, appreciation, a sense of purpose, love, and trust . . . all of which are made more powerful when based in the Spiritual realm. You would be wise to strengthen these supports step by step and day by day.

The exercises and ideas I have presented throughout give you a wonderful start on your Journey to truly embracing uncertainty . . . to helping you get to the place where you can say. . . .

"Bring it all on . . . I'm ready!"

So, jump right in. Actual experience is needed here. Some of the exercises may seem hard as they require changing long-held habits. But "hard" isn't necessarily bad. Poet and essayist John Ciardi told us that . . .

Every game ever invented by mankind, is a way of making things hard for the fun of it![1]

*Hard for the fun of it.* That's a great way to think about the exercises . . . and about life.

We all know that excellence in any sport or in the game of life itself doesn't come all at once. There are stops and starts and sometimes we topple over. But as we keep practicing, we can feel ourselves skimming the waves of life in an elegant fashion, knowing that we can go forward fully prepared to embrace the adventure of whatever lies before us. Heaven at last!

Remember that time is NOT of the essence. That's right. You don't have to rush, rush, rush. There is nowhere to "get to." You are on a lifelong Journey of Discovery and your task is simply to keep learning and growing all along the way. Spiritual changes take place . . .

S- - -L- - -O- - -W- - -L- - -Y.

Taking it s- -l- -o- -w- -l- -y allows you the time to look around, to be creative, thus allowing new insights to emerge. Just remember that . . .

All of life's creativity flourishes not in certainty, *but in the questions that flow from uncertainty.*

Today's world is filled with "quick" schemes for health, wealth, love, and all good things. Such quick schemes don't work, or at least I don't know of any that have worked.

Have patience. Impatience takes away joy. It tells you that you are wanting something that is somewhere else instead of focusing on the opportunity that exists in the here and now. When impatience rears its ugly head, just remember to move to a Higher place where you can cut the cord and say to yourself . . .

I let go and trust that it's all happening perfectly.

End of story. When you are desperately wanting something to happen, you lose sight of the fact that something IS happening. And if you learn and grow from it all, it truly is all happening perfectly!

Don't expect to "get it" for all times. On my own Spiritual Journey, I have attended many workshops, read many books, listened to many tapes, and experienced much of life, and on many occasions have felt . . . "Yes! I have it now." Wrong! I have it up to a certain point. And then life steps in and tells me it's time to move on and learn more. It's a Journey that lasts a lifetime.

Some of what life hands you will be wonderful and some will be difficult. There's no getting around the "difficult" part. But once you create the frame of mind that ALL that life offers is really a teacher of valuable lessons, it matters less, one way or the other . . . it's all about becoming a stronger and more loving person.

From the hard times, wonderful self-discoveries can be made. In fact, some would argue that huge advances are not possible without the hard times. The nature of life itself tells us that there will always be . . .

TIMES OF CONFUSION
which lead to
TIMES OF CLARITY
which lead to
TIMES OF CONFUSION
which lead to
TIMES OF CLARITY
which lead to
TIMES OF CONFUSION
which lead to
TIMES OF CLARITY

And so it goes.

Watch yourself unfold. Become the observer of your life instead of being trapped in the midst of the drama. When you are trapped in the drama, it is very hard to embrace the uncertainty. When you become the observer, you can be much more creative in discovering solutions to any situation or problem that comes your way.

As you watch yourself unfold, do it without judgment. Watch with an "Aha! Isn't that interesting?" state of mind. Life is a practice. You never get it totally right . . . but you do get to do it better. Appreciate the progress that is there. And just keep moving forward.

Experiment with it all, have fun, and stop berating yourself because you're not "there yet." I don't know anyone, even the best of our Spiritual teachers, who is "there yet." It is a lifelong process . . . for all of us.

Trust your power. When you trust your power, you trust the future. You *know* you can handle it all. To that end, it helps to find ways in which to build your mental and physical energy.

To illustrate, I jokingly gave myself the nickname, Storm. (You can now call me Storm Jeffers, as my friends laughingly do.) Ironically, it feels great. To me, it signifies my desire to shake things up a bit . . . to be a force for helping to change what doesn't work in this world.

I also enjoy Tae-Bo, a present-day form of the martial arts that makes me feel powerful. Yoga and meditation are very helpful for creating peace of mind; but there is also something wonderful about doing exercises that pull up our sense of power. Yes!

Being powerful does not mean trying to control people or events in your life; power is a state of consciousness. And what can feel more powerful than knowing you can handle whatever life brings you?

Trust that whatever you need will be there. And if it isn't, trust yourself to find it.

Remember that outcomes don't really matter in isolation. What matters is how you enjoy the process, the Journey, your life. What matters is how you thank your friends, how you appreciate the goodness in your life, how you take care of those you love and how you take pleasure in it all.

Lighten up. Play with life. Laugh a lot. I have a new philosophy . . .

If it's not funny, I can't take it seriously!

Don't take any of it . . . particularly yourself . . . too seriously.

So, world . . . bring it all on . . . we're ready to learn and grow. And I'll repeat what I told you about this book in the Introduction:

*This book definitely has a mind of its own.* It told me that it wants to be read over and over again. It wants to be your resource when you need help in pushing through your worries about the future. It wants to help you in a multitude of ways. So make this book one of your very best friends. Visit it often and get to know it well. If you do, it won't let you down.

"Okay, Susan, it's really time for you to end this book."
And so it is. And I end it with much love . . .

From my heart to yours,

*Susan (Storm) Jeffers*

# Embracing the Exercises!

Here is a list of the exercises in all their glory with the page numbers included. Pick the ones that have "spoken" to you as you have made your way through the book and embrace them as an essential and enjoyable part of your life.

# Notes

Many of the following books quoted throughout are a valuable part of my library, and I refer to them and cite them frequently. Some of them are quite old and will no longer be in print. Also, over time, some of the following website addresses may change or disappear. Not to worry, however. There is always another book, website, or other resource out there to provide you with exactly what you need. Just keep looking.

## INTRODUCTION

1. Cooper, Walter. *Shards: Restoring the Tattered Spirit.* Health Communications, Inc., Deerfield Beach, FL, 1992, p. 5.

2. Watts, Alan W. *The Wisdom of Insecurity: A Message for an Age of Anxiety.* Vintage Books, a division of Random House, New York, 1951, pp. 14–15.

## CHAPTER 1

1. Goldman, Francisco. "The Magical Realism of the Elian Chronicle," *Los Angeles Times*, April 20, 2000, p. M2.

## CHAPTER 2

1. This quote appeared in the "Proust Questionnaire" in *Vanity Fair*, July, 2000, p. 200. (For those of you who may not know, Sting is

a brilliant pop star formerly of the band, Police. He presently performs solo.)

2. Found in *Fire in the Soul: A New Psychology of Spiritual Optimism* by Joan Borysenko, Ph.D., Warner Books, 1993, page 15.

3. Found in *Burst Out Laughing*, Celestial Arts, Berkeley, CA 1984, p. 20. In her entertaining books, Barry Stevens discusses her study and practice of Gestalt therapy, the methods of Zen, Krishnamurti, and the American Indian as they helped her push through the difficulties in life.

4. Feynman, Richard P. *The Meaning of It All: Thoughts of a Citizen-Scientist.* Perseus Books, Reading, Massachusetts, 1998, p. 28.

5. Fields, Rick, with Peggy Taylor, Rex Weyler, and Rick Ingrasci. *Chop Wood, Carry Water: A Guide to Finding Spiritual Fulfillment in Everyday Life.* Jeremy P. Tarcher, Inc., Los Angeles, 1984, p. 8.

6. To learn more about Chungliang Al Huang and Tai Ji, read *Embrace Tiger, Return to Mountain: The Essence of Tai Ji*, Celestial Arts, Berkeley, CA 1973, 1987.

7. Hallstein, Richard W. *Memoirs of a Recovering Autocrat: Revealing Insights for Managing the Autocrat in All of Us.* Berrett-Koehler, San Francisco, 1992, p. 21.

8. One of my favorite books on the subject of Aikido and resolving conflict is *The Magic of Conflict* by Thomas F. Crum. A Touchstone Book, Simon and Schuster, New York, 1987.

9. *I'm Okay . . . You're a Brat: Setting the Priorities Straight and Freeing You from the Guilt and Mad Myths of Parenthood.* Renaissance Books: (Distributed by St. Martin's Press), 1999.

CHAPTER 3

1. The need for control starts very young as you can see from twelve-year old Julie's insightful letter. I thank her father, Jerry Beckerman for showing it to me and I thank Julie for giving me permission to use it.

2. Found in *Developing Inward Calm*, the ninth in a series of twenty-one printed lectures given by Dr. Bernard Jensen, D.C., N.D., a nutritionist and chiropractor. Bernard Jensen Products, Publishing Division, Solana Beach, CA, 1976, p. 10.

3. Stevens, Barry. *Burst Out Laughing*. Celestial Arts, Berkeley, CA, 1984, p. 35.

4. Crum, Thomas. *The Magic of Conflict*. A Touchstone Book, Simon and Schuster, New York, 1987, p. 15.

5. Jeffers, Susan. *Opening Our Hearts to Men: Taking Charge of our Lives and Creating a Love that Works*. A Fawcett Columbine Book, Published by Ballantine Books, NY, 1989, p. 191.

## CHAPTER 4

1. Wilde, Stuart. *Miracles*. Wisdom Books, Inc., Taos, NM, 1983, p. 7.

2. Vaughan, Frances E. *Awakening Intuition*. Anchor Books, Garden City, New York, 1979, page 4.

3. Schulz, M.D., Ph.D., Mona Lisa, *Awakening Intuition: Using Your Mind-Body Network for Insight and Healing*. Harmony Books, New York, 1998, p. 6.

4. During the ten years I was the executive director of the Floating Hospital, it was a health, educational, and recreational facility for the poor in New York City actually located aboard a ship. In the summer months, it sailed around Manhattan with eight hundred passengers and over 115 staff members aboard. The fact that it was aboard a ship made all the passengers "captive" to the many programs available throughout the day. In the winter months, it conducted its programs dockside. It has been over twenty years since I left the Floating Hospital to pursue my present career and its programs may have changed in the interim.

5. Chopra, Deepak. *Creating Affluence: Wealth Consciousness in the Field of All Possibilities*. New World Library, 58 Paul Drive, San Rafael, CA 94903, 1993. (Audiotape)

6. See *Feel the Fear and Do It Anyway, Feel the Fear and Beyond,* and *End the Struggle and Dance with Life.*

7. Koch-Sheras, Ph.D., Phyllis R., Amy Lemley, and Peter L. Sheras, Ph.D. *The Dream Sourcebook and Journal: A Guide to the Theory and Interpretation of Dreams.* Barnes & Noble Books, 1995, 1996, 1998.

8. Huson, Paul. *How to Test and Develop Your ESP.* Madison Books, New York, 2001. (Originally published in 1975 by Stein and Day, New York.)

9. A Course in Miracles (Volume 2) Workbook for Students, Foundation for Inner Peace, P.O. Box 635, Tiburon, CA 94920, 1975, p. 121.

10. *Seven Taoist Masters: A Folk Novel of China.* Translated by Eva Wong. Shambhala Publications, Boston, 1990, p. 45.

CHAPTER 5

1. Found in *The Little Zen Companion* by David Schiller, Workman Publishing, New York, 1994, p. 147.

2. Silverman, Robin. *The Ten Gifts: Find the Personal Peace You've Always Wanted Through the Ten Gifts You've Always Had.* St. Martin's Press, New York, 2000, p. xvii.

3. Al Gore ceded the presidency of the United States to George W. Bush on Dec 13, 2000.

4. Wingate. *Tilling the Soul.* Aurora Press, New York, 1984, p. 83.

5. Briggs, John and F. David Peat. *Seven Life Lessons of Chaos: Timeless Wisdom from the Science of Change.* HarperCollins, New York, 1999, p. 2.

CHAPTER 6

1. Watts, Alan W. *The Meaning of Happiness: The Quest for Freedom of the Spirit in Modern Psychology and the Wisdom of the East.* Harper and Row Publishers, New York, 1940, 1968, p. 197.

2. I encourage every one of you to read or reread Viktor Frankl's life-changing book, *Man's Search for Meaning*. (Pocket Books, New York, 1939, 1963.)

3. Ibid., p. 56.

4. Ibid., p. 60.

5. Ibid., p. 104.

6. Dass, Ram. *Still Here: Embracing Aging, Changing, and Dying*. Riverhead Books, New York, 2000.

7. Ibid., p. 185.

8. Ibid., pp. 188 and 202.

9. Ibid., p. 6

10. Ibid., pp. 190–191.

11. From a talk at the Open Secret Bookstore in San Rafael, April 21, 1999.

12. Ibid., p. 197.

13. Ibid., pp. 196–197.

14. Ibid., p. 198.

15. You can visit the Ram Dass website at HYPERLINK "http://www.ramdasstapes.org." There you will be able to learn more about Ram Dass and order from his large collection of tapes and books.

16. Vaughn, Susan. "Motivational Speaker's Dreams Were Detoured but Not Lost," *Los Angeles Times*, March 18, 2001, Work Place Section (W), pp. 1–2.

17. You can learn more about this important Foundation by visiting HYPERLINK "http://www.pollyklaas.org" and HYPERLINK "http://www.klaaskids.org."

18. To learn more read "Find Beauty in the Land of Tears" in *End the Struggle and Dance with Life*, Chapter 9.

19. If you're curious as to what blessings I could possibly find in breast cancer, you can read my acceptance speech for this wonderful award in *Feel the Fear . . . and Beyond*, Chapter 3.

CHAPTER 7

1. Frankl, Viktor. *Man's Search for Meaning*. Pocket Books, New York, 1939, 1963, p. 93.

2. As heard on the television show *60 Minutes*. (CBS, April 2, 2000.)

3. Castaneda, Carlos. *The Teachings of Don Juan: A Yaqui Way of Knowledge*. Pocket Books, New York, 1968, 1998, p. 75.

4. If you are interested in learning more about The Land of Tears, I again refer you to Chapter 9 in *End the Struggle and Dance with Life* entitled "Find Beauty in the Land of Tears."

CHAPTER 8

1. Found in *The Great Thoughts*. Compiled by George Seldes. Ballantine Books, 1985, p. 390.

2. Found in *The Wheel of Life and Death* by Philip Kapleau, The Zen Center (a New York not-for-profit religious corporation), New York, 1989, p. 70.

3. As heard in Ram Dass and Stephen Levine's videotape *Exploring the Heart of Healing: An exploration of our healing into life within the context of our experience of dying*, The Access Group, Novato, CA, 1988.

4. Dass, Ram. *Still Here: Embracing Aging, Changing, and Dying*. Riverhead Books, New York, 2000, pp. 165–166.

5. Morse, Melvin L. with Paul Perry. *Closer to the Light*, Fawcett, New York, 1992. You can visit his website at HYPERLINK "http://www.melvinmorse.com."

6. The International Association for Near-Death Studies (IANDS), P.O. Box 502, East Windsor Hill, CT 06028, HYPERLINK "http://www.iands.org."

7. Prather, Hugh. *There Is a Place Where You Are Not Alone*. A Dolphin Book, Doubleday, 1980, p. 35.

CHAPTER 9

1. Chogyam Trungpa, *Shambhala: The Sacred Path of the Warrior*. Bantam Books, New York, 1984, p. 29.

2. Ryan, Richard M. and Edward L. Deci. "On Happiness and Human Potentials: A Review of Research on Hedonic and Eudaimonic Well-Being." *Annual Review of Psychology*, 2001, p. 4.

3. Caldwell, Christopher. "Anybody Having Fun," *TALK MAGAZINE*, August 2000, p. 25.

4. Ibid., p. 25.

5. This wonderful "misquote" was found in *The Tao of Pooh: In which The Way is revealed by the Bear of Little Brain* by Benjamin Hoff, A Mandarin Paperback, London, 1982, p. 77.

6. *Seven Taoist Masters: A Folk Novel of China*. Translated by Eva Wong. Shambhala Publications, Boston, 1990, p. 74.

CHAPTER 10

1. Source Unknown.

2. I suggest you read the beautifully illustrated and moving book *The Illuminated Rumi*. Translations and Commentary by Coleman Barks, Illuminations by Michael Green, Broadway Books, 1997.

3. Matthew Fox tells this story on his audiotape *Exploring the Cosmic Christ Archetype, Part 1,* Sounds True Recordings, 735 Walnut Street, Boulder, CO 80302.

4. Prather, Hugh. *There Is a Place Where You Are Not Alone.* A Dolphin Book, Doubleday, 1980, p. 35.

5. "God Diagnosed With Bipolar Disorder" in *The Onion,* May 2, 2001. HYPERLINK "http://www.theonion.com."

6. Larry Dossey, M.D. provides compelling evidence about the power of prayer in *Healing Words: The Power of Prayer and the Practice of Medicine*. HarperSanFrancisco, 1993.

7. *End the Struggle and Dance with Life*, p. 181.

## CHAPTER 11

1. Glassner, Barry. *The Culture of Fear*. Basic Books, New York, 1999, p. xxi.

2. Ibid., p. xxi.

3. Dr. Renata Mihalic is the founder of Purple Aura Chiropractic in Los Angeles, CA.

4. Dr. Mihalic created her technique after studying the Bio Energetic Synchronization Technique (B.E.S.T.), Human Energy Field Research at UCLA, Chi Kung (Qigong), Reiki, Sound Healing and Universal Ministry.

5. Morter, Dr. M. Ted, Jr. *Dynamic Health: Using Your Own Beliefs, Thoughts and Memory to Create a Healthy Body*, Morter HealthSystems, 1000 West Poplar Street, Rogers, Arkansas 72756, revised 1997 and Guyton, Arthur C. Textbook of Medical Physiology, 8th edition, W.B. Saunders Company, Philadelphia.

6. Alain. *On Happiness*. Frederick Ungar Publishing Company, New York, 1928, 1973, p. 29.

## CHAPTER 12

1. Jeffers, Susan. *Feel the Fear and Do It Anyway: Dynamic Techniques for Turning Fear, Indecision and Anger into Power, Action, and Love*. Fawcett Columbine, New York, 1986, p. 16.

2. Marilyn Furguson is the author of *The Aquarian Conspiracy: Personal and Social Transformation in the 1980s*. J.P. Tarcher, Los Angeles, 1980.

3. Yes, that's the title of his entertaining book! *Shift Happens!: Powerful Ways to Transform Your Life* by Robert Holden, Hodder & Stoughton, London, 2000.

EPILOGUE

1. This quote was found on the Internet. John Ciardi was a poet, essayist, translator. During the last decade of his life, he won great popularity as a radio commentator on National Public Radio. He died in 1986.

# ABOUT THE AUTHOR

SUSAN JEFFERS, PH.D. continues to help millions of people throughout the world overcome their fears, heal their relationships, and move forward in life with confidence and love. She is the author of many books and tapes including the best-selling *Feel the Fear and Do It Anyway, Feel the Fear . . . and Beyond, End the Struggle and Dance with Life,* and *Opening Our Hearts to Men.* Dr. Jeffers is also a popular public speaker and media personality. She lives with her husband, Mark Shelmerdine, in Los Angeles. Her website address is www.susanjeffers.com.